Pine River and Lone Peak

PINE RIVER AND LONE PEAK

An Anthology of

Three Chosŏn Dynasty Poets

Translated,

with an Introduction,

by Peter H. Lee

University of Hawaii Press

Honolulu

© 1991 University of Hawaii Press
All Rights Reserved
Printed in the United States of America
91 93 94 95 96 97 5 4 3 2 1

Library of Congress Cataloging-in-Publication Data

Pine River and lone peak : an anthology of three Chosŏn
    dynasty poets / translated, with an introduction, by
    Peter H. Lee.
        p.   cm.
    Translations of sixteenth-century Korean poetry.
    Includes bibliographical references and index.
    ISBN 0–8248–1298–0 (alk. paper)
        1. Korean poetry—16th century—Translations into English.
    2. English poetry—Translations from Korean. I. Lee,
    Peter H., 1929–   .
    PL984.E3P56   1991
    895.7'1208—dc20   90–44433
                                                           CIP

A Study from the Center for Korean Studies,
University of Hawaii

The Center for Korean Studies was established in 1972 to coordinate
and develop the resources for the study of Korea at the University of
Hawaii. Its goals are to enhance faculty quality and performance in
Korean studies; to develop comprehensive, balanced academic pro-
grams; to stimulate research and publications; and to coordinate the
resources of the University of Hawaii with those of other institutions,
organizations, and individual scholars engaged in the study of Korea.
Reflecting the diversity of the academic disciplines represented by af-
filiated members of the University faculty, the Center seeks especially
to promote interdisciplinary and intercultural studies.

University of Hawaii Press books are printed
on acid-free paper and meet the guidelines
for permanence and durability of the Council
on Library Resources

CONTENTS

PREFACE

The three poets of the Chosŏn dynasty making up this anthology have been generally valued for their contributions to classical Korean poetry—Chŏng Ch'ŏl (1537–1594) for his *kasa* and *sijo,* Pak Illo (1561–1643) for his *kasa,* and Yun Sŏndo (1587–1671) for his *sijo.* Although sixteenth- and seventeenth-century Korean is relatively close to the modern spoken language, the diction, social and literary conventions, thematic sequences, structural patterns, tone, and rhetorical topics often need explanation. Indeed, in spite of these poets' colloquial directness, we do not belong to their immediate audience. More important, certain dramatic situations and emotional implications, readily accessible to a select readership of the times, may remain baffling to the modern reader. Poems cast as romantic complaints with the speaker as an abandoned lady, for example, are written in the tradition of "Encountering Sorrow" of Ch'ü Yüan and his imitators in which the exiled courtier longs for his sovereign and pours out his pathetic grief. Poems written to praise the retreat of a patron or friend usually combine encomiastic and eremetic motifs, topographical and moral, or Confucian and Taoist, or any combination of these. And the moral vision presented in the Neo-Confucian didactic poems, with their freighted content and serious purpose, may appear grave and gloomy in the current moral climate.

Readable as their language seems, the poems abound with cryptic personal references and lexical ambiguities. Allusions to the Chinese canonical works, usually cast in Chinese graphs to satisfy the metrical requirements—intertextuality called for by an urge to say much in little—are worked into the translations whenever possible. Certain proper nouns, such as the names of mountains, rivers, waterfalls, and edifices, are, whenever possible, also translated for the benefit of the reader who is likely to miss their meanings in the romanization. Throughout I have attempted to reproduce the number of lines in the original. My line constitutes two metric segments, usually divided by a caesura. (Each segment comprises from two to seven syllables, commonly three or four.) Traditionally, four segments make up a line.

I have used some paragraphs from my *Celebration of Continuity: Themes in Classic East Asian Poetry* (Cambridge: Harvard University Press, 1979).

I wish to thank my students who have read Chŏng Ch'ŏl and Yun Sŏndo with me at UCLA for teaching me the difficulty of translating their works, Forrest R. Pitts and Don Yoder for their valuable suggestions, and the Korean Culture and Arts Foundation for encouragement.

My deepest gratitude is to my family.

Introduction

Neo-Confucianist in its official political and moral philosophy, the Chosŏn dynasty coincided with the Confucian revival in Korean history. The teachings of the Ch'eng-Chu school—a syncretic philosophy encompassing all aspects of life—were imported to the country in the beginning of the fourteenth century, and the last years of the Koryŏ dynasty saw the emergence of several great thinkers, some of whom helped in the founding of the new dynasty. As architects of the new political and economic order, they ascribed the fall of Koryŏ to Buddhism and declared Neo-Confucianism to be the guiding ideology of the new kingdom.[1] Once their control had been secured, the meritorious elite monopolized power and wealth and indulged in literary pursuits. This trend became more prominent among the supporters of King Sejo's usurpation (1455), and they virtually monopolized the civil service examination—the most respected avenue for entry to officialdom and the bureaucracy.

The Neo-Confucian literati in the provinces, who shared common interests and aspirations, bided their time for an opportunity to put their political and moral vision into practice. As agricultural landowners, they strengthened their status by the local agency, the village compact, and private academies.[2] The curriculum in village schools and academies was geared to the civil service examination, but it emphasized the Confucian classics, especially the *Elementary Learning (Hsiao-hsüeh)*, and the actual implementation of the sage's teachings. Committed to the Confucian Way and the fulfillment of man's moral character, the Neo-Confucian literati in the provinces sought a balance between moral and intellectual education and aimed at achieving sagehood through self-cultivation. They believed that the best way of challenging the entrenched meritorious elite was to master the teachings of the Sung masters and adhere strictly to principles. Thus cosmological and epistemological inquiry deepened as they became more active from the late fifteenth century.

I

The emergence of the Neo-Confucian literati through the route of examination brought about a reform in the examination system itself, as more emphasis was given to the classics. Some scorned as "spurious art" the verse and prose compositions that had hitherto comprised the bulk of the examination and insisted that emphasis on literary skills led to a utilitarian exploitation of classical learning, but not to the renewal or practice of it in one's own day.[3] They also tried to restrain the political monopoly of the ruling elite. The more powerful the meritorious elite, the stronger the ties between the king and the rising Neo-Confucian literati. Threatened with the loss of their hegemony, the meritorious elite began to persecute their opponents. But the rise of the new literati was inevitable. Based on a foundation of Neo-Confucian education and ideology, Chosŏn society was built on a rivalry among the educated, and the purges could not stop the rising literati who had a strong economic and educational base in the provinces.

The power struggle between the meritorious elite and the rising Neo-Confucian literati brought about four purges (1498, 1504, 1519, and 1545).[4] With each purge, the literati suffered a serious setback but did not abandon their effort to consolidate power. The reason for this factional strife lay in the limited job market for the literati. With the spread of education that accompanied the rise of Neo-Confucianism in Korea, the number of degree holders increased but not the positions they could fill in the capital and provinces.

In 1575 a personal feud between two officials, Sim Ŭigyŏm (1535–1587) and Kim Hyowŏn (1532–1590), over appointments to key positions in the Ministry of Personnel led to full-fledged strife.[5] The positions in question were not only stepping stones to further advancement but controlled the recommendation, selection, and dismissal of officials. When Kim Hyowŏn, who placed first in the examination, was recommended for that post, Sim Ŭigyŏm, younger brother of the reigning queen, accused him of opportunism. Kim did obtain the post, however, and when his successor was to be named, Sim's younger brother emerged as a worthy candidate. Kim took the opportunity to settle old scores, and officials began to side with one or the other. Kim's faction was called the Easterners, because Kim lived in the eastern part of Seoul, below Camel Mountain, while Sim's faction was termed the Westerners because Sim lived in the western side, the modern Chŏngdong area. After the death of the moderator Yi I in 1584, the Easterners seized power but were replaced by the Westerners five years later. In 1591 the Easterners again emerged victorious. The radicals among the Easterners were called the Northerners, while the moderates were styled the Southerners.

Factional politics involved not only protagonists but their descendants and clansmen as well. A temporary setback did not discourage partisans, who, out of filial piety, would bide their time to avenge the wrongs done to their ancestors. Teachers in the private academies would indoctrinate students in their ideology, and students, once employed, tended to view public issues through their factional affiliation. The Easterners wielded power in 1584–1589 and 1591–1623 (Northerners), while the Westerners prevailed in 1589–1591, 1623–1674, 1680–1689, and 1694–1724. The Southerners were strong only in 1674–1680 and 1689–1694. Schools of Neo-Confucian metaphysics were also drawn in. The Easterners included pupils of Yi Hwang (1501–1571) and Cho Sik (1501–1572), for example, and the Westerners those of Yi I (1536–1584) and Sŏng Hon (1535–1598). From the moment of birth one was regarded as an enemy by his opposing faction. Members of opposing factions seldom intermarried or shared the same table. Their verbal battles, spectacles of rhetorical virtuosity, were not waged over social reform or public welfare but such ritual issues as the period of mourning for members of the royal family or the selection of the crown prince. Parochial and cliquish, the educated elite justified their existence by persuading the throne to side with their cause and branding others as disloyal or seditious.

POETIC CODES AND CULTURAL NORMS

The political career of the poet Chŏng Ch'ŏl, a Westerner, was spent during the dominance of the Easterners. After an unsuccessful attempt to reconcile the two factions in 1578, a reply he composed to a petition submitted by the prime minister at royal order was construed as an impeachment of the latter (1581).[6] His proposal of Prince Kwanghae as successor displeased the king, and his opponents rushed to denounce him for his misjudgment and exiled him (1591).[7] More than once (1583, 1591), Chŏng was termed unfit to serve owing to his fondness for wine. He was released only when, during the king's flight north to escape the advancing Japanese army in 1592, an old man came forward and entreated the king for his pardon.[8] An Minhak praises Chŏng in his memorial address: "His appearance was that of a pine crowned with clouds, while his resoluteness was like a snow-capped bamboo."[9] The pine and bamboo are two of the favorite emblematic plants in Confucian moral rhetoric; he was generally considered "loyal, filial, upright, and honest," but his colleagues found him wanting in tolerance and magnanimity.[10]

As a Southerner, the poet Yun Sŏndo's political career was thorny. Known as a man of courage and integrity, Yun often stunned the court by his memorials denouncing this or that powerful minister as corrupt. The first such memorial earned him exile of seven years in the northeast (1616–1623).[11] His candid criticism of current affairs so disturbed some courtiers that he was forced to flee to his retreat (1644, 1649).[12] If he did not accept an offer from the court, he was denounced for disobedience and exiled (1638)[13] or called arrogant (1652, 1658).[14] If the king wanted him, his enemies schemed to prevent his appointment (1649). His choice of a site for King Hyojong's tomb[15] and his proposal of a three-year mourning period for the queen mother[16] earned him another seven years' exile (1660–1667).[17] Yun's political career spanned the reigns of four kings—Kwanghaegun, Injo, Hyojong, and Hyŏnjong. Yun spent a full fourteen years in exile, but the Westerners' calumny and high-handedness seldom affected his integrity. In Yun's tomb inscription Hŏ Mok (1595–1682) compares him to Pi Kan, an uncle of Chou Hsin (r. 1154–1122 B.C.), the last wicked ruler of Shang, who allowed his nephew the tyrant to cut open his heart; to Po I, who disapproved of the conquest by King Wu of Chou Hsin and retired to Shou-yang Mountain and died of starvation; and to Ch'ü Yüan, a loyal minister to King Huai of Ch'u, who was rewarded with slander and banishment and drowned himself in the Milo River.[18] "The more he was straightened, the harder his resolution became, and he was unbowed at death's door." Such was the estimate of a contemporary.

Why should a piece of paper—a memorial—send one to a remote no-man's-land with unpalatable diet and insufferable discomfort? For a courtier, the memorial was a common means of speaking out on a public issue, perhaps the next best thing to an open debate in the presence of the king. It might take the form of a philosophical, political, or moral debate in which the opponent was either mentioned or alluded to—a kind of silent symposium replete with classical precedents and allusions. It might contain biting gibes and taunts, but the more vehement the tone, the more disruptive its effect. Usually it was composed with considerable sophistication, structure, and rhetoric—balanced phrases, pleasing asymmetry, antithesis, exclamations, rhetorical questions—all the while observing unwritten rules and decorum. Undisguised aggression or personal hostility were taboo, however, for the opponent could match insult with insult. As a means of expressing one's passion and energy, memorial writing might have been satisfying, but it was not always safe. The writer might lose his life for it. When the evils of the court reached appalling heights in the late sixteenth and early seventeenth centuries, the memorial often touched on the opponent's overreaching ambition, unscrupulous greed, or shameless opportunism. It then could be easily construed as slander or defamation, and the quid pro quo exchange might result in trumped-up charges.

The poets Chŏng Ch'ŏl (who wrote five memorials) and Yun Sŏndo (who wrote twenty-eight memorials) acutely felt the discrepancy between the ideals and realities of courtly life and vented their frustrations in undisguised attacks on their opponents. Lacking moderation and humor, both used the memorial as a means to attack and degrade their enemies. The outcome was predictable. No wonder they repeatedly declare that their path to happiness is not through ambition and design but a simple rural life free from the afflictions of worry and responsibility. Hence the popularity of seclusion. The courtier's obsession with the perplexing world of politics—and sudden falls from high places—led these poets to create a counterideology, a romantic mythology of pure countryside, a maternal and benign landscape, thus transforming a poetry of reclusion into a poetry of protest. To them it was an affirmation of spirit—and poetry—over chaos and absurdity.

Exile was the usual punishment for the courtier. Many famous writers in East Asia spent some time as exiles or unemployed lumpen-intelligentsia. The frequent use of exile in political vendettas seems to indicate that power holders were not prepared to suffer opposition or criticism. The distance the offender was removed from the capital was a measure of the gravity of the offense. If one was transported to tundra or a lonely island to fend for himself—at times even begging for his own food—it meant that his opponents did not want him to return alive. Banishment meant isolation. Cut off from the center of power and culture and the community of civilized men, a political enemy deserved to suffer the desolation of loneliness—or so it was thought when party strife was rampant. The courtier, the gentleman trained in Confucian humanism, represented tradition, authority, privilege, legitimacy, and order. Once displaced and isolated, he lost touch with everything vital, dynamic, and creative. In a culture where only the king could make or unmake the courtier, lying low in the wilderness while awaiting a pardon or summons represented a life of anguish.

Chŏng Ch'ŏl and Yun Sŏndo, however, made use of adversity as a trial of spirit. As the exiled Duke Senior muses in the forest of Arden (*As You Like It*, 2.1.12–17):

> Sweet are the uses of adversity,
> Which, like the toad, ugly and venomous,
> Wears yet a precious jewel in his head:
> And this our life, exempt from public haunt,
> Finds tongues in trees, books in the running brooks,
> Sermons in stone, and good in every thing.

Two poems by Chŏng Ch'ŏl on the theme of constancy written during his voluntary reclusion, for example, were praised by his contemporaries as perfect examples of patience and fortitude.[19] They find in them a poet speaking with such individual style and such strength of spirit and dignity that his virtue is never overcome by ill fortune. The reader detects the principles of culture operating here, a mirror of its time. For these poets, exile spurred their creativity and brought out the best in them. Whether they were in their retreat or places of exile, they seldom gave up writing. This also explains the polemical stance

and the intrusion of politics in much of their poetry and the deep influ-
ence their political career exercised on their poetic development.

This leads us to the question of poetry's place in society and culture.
While Western theories of literature begin with the discussion of
drama, East Asia begins with lyric poetry. The *Book of Songs,* the ear-
liest anthology of poetry in China, was one of the original five canoni-
cal texts. Poetry was taught and examined at the national academy in
China and in Korea. Produced on every conceivable occasion, poetry
was a common means of communication between officials, diplomats,
friends, and lovers. If a member of the lower classes—a soldier, mer-
chant, or slave—is mentioned at all in history, it is because of his abil-
ity to write poetry, especially in Chinese. In such a setting, none could
dispute the place of poetry in society and culture. Indeed, even tyrants
left poems, and kings themselves wrote. While they may not have
regarded poetry as their vocation (though to do so would not have
been incompatible with courtly values), few kings were enjoined from
indulging in verse as an avocation. Surrounded by learned poets, the
king often found poetry instructive, delightful, and persuasive. Many
persons won favor by poetry; not being able to produce a poem on
command was considered a great disgrace. Indeed, it is no exaggera-
tion to say that the cultural role played by the orator in the West was
played in Chosŏn dynasty Korea by the *doctus poeta.* Yu Hoin (1445–
1494), King Sŏngjong's favorite courtier, won royal favor with his
poetic gifts. When Yu had to leave the court to care for his ailing
mother, the king wrote him the following poem in Korean:

> Stay:
> Will you go? Must you go?
> Is it in weariness that you go? From disgust?
> Who advised you? Who persuaded you?
> Say why you are leaving.
> You, who are breaking my heart.[20]

(Despite the strong ties between the two men, the king never
appointed Yu to a post he could not manage and thus won the admira-
tion of posterity.)

Education to a Korean writer in the fifteenth and sixteenth centuries meant a study of the language and literature of classical China. Chinese poetry was the only poetry seriously studied and imitated. Writers knew how to make use of literary resources of the tradition; they also knew how to engage the lively concerns of the age. They all desired to use words rich in literary and historical connotations, resonant with verbal echoes. Precedent offered not only freedom but modes of expression. In fact, every good writer exploited the reader's knowledge of the original. Lu Chi says, "A pithy saying at a crucial point / may whip all parts into a whole."[21] A mixture of vernacular and Chinese, classical and modern, was second nature to these poets.

The importance of memorization in classical education is well known. A student usually recited his texts aloud until he had committed them to memory. By listening to their young masters reciting, even slaves and servants were often able to learn scraps of classical Chinese. The Korean culture of the day revered not only the written word but the spoken word as well. Memory helped a writer to recall the world of the classics while organizing his own thoughts. It was a testimony to his powers of concentration, to his correct understanding of the texts, to his ability to use the "places" in such texts at will, to make the difficult appear easy, and to use examples to present his argument effectively. The literary miscellany recounts feats of prodigious memory. While on night duty, Ku Chongjik (1424–1477) made an unauthorized visit to Kyŏnghoe Tower, where he met King Sŏngjong taking a walk. At the king's request, Ku recited the *Spring and Autumn Annals* from memory. The following day the king appointed him censor-general.[22] Kim Mun (d. 1448) and Yun Ki could recite everything in the *Outline and Digest of the General Mirror (T'ung-chien kang-mu).*[23] Particularly impressive was Chŏng Ch'o (d. 1434), who could memorize a book in a single reading. A few days before an examination, he glanced at the classics and passed with flying colors. As a boy he bet a monk that he could memorize the *Diamond Scripture* in one reading. The monk lost the bet and fled.[24] Im Wŏnjun (1423–1500) could remember the names of five hundred female entertainers after a single glance at the official roster.[25] Like Niceratus' feat of repeating from memory the entire *Iliad* and *Odyssey* (as reported by Xenophon) or the Yugoslavian *guslar*'s reputed knowledge of 100,000 verses,[26] these feats astonish the modern reader, who has lost much of his power of memory and can no longer recognize allusions to the classics without numerous footnotes.

The art of the poet's compositional technique illustrates the workings of poetic memory. Poets not only assume the reader's literary competence, his knowledge of the conventions of the traditional poetic forms, *sijo* and *kasa,* but his ability to recall quotations from and allusions to exemplary texts. Both memory and allusion contribute to the "process of poetic signification as constitutive elements of poetic discourse."[27] Memory helps the poet to engage in a continuous dialogue with his tradition that provides him with motifs, topoi, imagery, and settings. He uses inherited codes and rules and models his voice and gestures on those of his most admired predecessors. In his poem he endeavors to strike a balance between his need to express himself and his desire to create a work of art. To introduce something new was to return to the old. Thus, the poet extends his tradition by selecting his material and arranging it in new patterns in a constant interplay between model and imitation. Allusion is an integral part of the literary system, and the reader is expected to know the historicity of codes and words as well as their diachronic itinerary.

If memory was the thesaurus of poetry, the use of allusion was the guiding impulse of poetic creation.[28] The simplest instance of allusion is the use of proper nouns—persons, places, titles, and the like. In "The Wanderings," for example, Chŏng Ch'ŏl invokes Chi Ch'ang-ju, Lin Pu, Mount Lu, Mounts Tung and T'ai, Three Days Cove, and the *Book of the Yellow Court,* to name but a few referents. Personal names require knowledge of individual lives and deciding what to associate with a given name;[29] place-names require knowledge of the original contexts in which they were used, settings and associations. The poet activates each of these allusions to "promote the coherence" of a work and "validate the autonomy of poetic discourse."[30]

Another type of allusion is the use of quotations—in exact or different order—from the Chinese classics and poetry. The appearance of orotund Chinese doublets or four-word phrases amid Korean words at once signals the reader what their functions are. Such quotations impart strong stress and a rich sonorific texture and usually lead to emphasis. In his *kasa* and moral verse Pak Illo delights in quoting such four-word phrases from the Confucian canon to invest his works with authority and impart the intended tone and meaning. The authority of the canon, the requisite of formal curriculum in his day, was still alive, irreplaceable, and quotable.

Furthermore, the use of four-word phrases of Chinese origin was called for by the formal restrictions of the *sijo* and *kasa* whenever a four-syllable Korean equivalent could not be found. A skillful use of such phrases contributed not only to poetic amplification but to the rhythm of a poem—the tetrameter line being the basic meter of the *sijo* and *kasa*. It was Yi Chonyŏn (1268–1342) who introduced the four-word phrase of Chinese origin in the first group of the second line, because no Korean equivalent could convey the tone and dignity and concision of the expression. Such brilliant focusing on a particular word or phrase abounds in good poems.

Chŏng Ch'ŏl offers instances of well-amalgamated allusions. In

> noble birds in white and black silk
> soar into midair . . .

the four-word phrase *hoŭi hyŏnsang* (here translated as "white and black silk") is an allusion in reverse order to Su Shih's "The Red Cliff, 2," where Su says, "It [a lone crane] wore a black robe and a coat of white silk."[31] Chŏng's playful allusion, while acknowledging his indebtedness to the Chinese poet, is so well integrated the reader might overlook it. A more difficult allusion for the untutored reader occurs when Chŏng ends "Continued Hymn of Constancy" with two lines:

> kaksinim tariya khaniwa   "The moon say you, my lady?
> kujŭnbi na toesyosyŏ   Rather, a driving rain."

When the first lady wishes to be a moon to allay the pangs of her unrequited love, the second suggests that she would rather be "a driving rain." Since these two lines are in pure Korean, the allusion is less readily apparent. "A driving rain" *(kujŭnbi)* is an allusion to the "Rhymeprose on Kao-t'ang," attributed to Sung Yü, wherein the goddess who appeared to King Hsiang of Ch'u in an erotic dream says,

"At dawn I am the morning cloud, and at dusk, the driving rain." The second lady's wish is more realistic—what she desires is physical union.

CHŎNG CH'ŎL

All Korean poets who passed the civil service examination wrote poems in Chinese. The three poets examined here are no exception, but they also wrote in Korean in the two enduring forms of vernacular poetry, the *sijo* and the *kasa*. They did so not for prestige but for their own art and pleasure, perhaps chanting them among friends when they got together. *Sijo* and *kasa* poems seldom brought prestige, advancement, or power. Chŏng Ch'ŏl's *kasa* poems were written in the 1580s, the most productive decade of his life. They were very popular in his day, and his contemporaries ranked him first among the *kasa* poets of the Chosŏn dynasty. In "The Wanderings" (*Kwandong pyŏlgok*, 1580) the poet narrates his journey from Seoul to the Inner Diamond Mountains and then describes his joy at observing, contemplating, and describing scenes famous for their beauty and magnificence. The reader is presented with a continuous unfolding of scenes described from various perspectives, encompassing both the sky and the sea, engaging all the senses. Chŏng's impressive structure and proportion evince his originality, especially compared with a number of poems on the same subject by a host of writers before him and after. A harmonious blending of scenes and historical reflection drawing on Chinese and Korean tradition adds to the richness, built upon the reader's ability to recognize verbal echoes. The poem's impelling rhythm comes from a mixture of colloquial and learned diction, a controlled language with balance, parallelism, antithesis, and symmetry.

Chŏng's bold description shows great skill in conveying a magnificent scene of nature in simple but carefully chosen words, avoiding the usual simile, as he transforms waterfalls at Myriad Falls Grotto into silver rainbows and the furious motion of whales:

> There silver rainbows,
> dragons with jade tails,

> turning and coiling, spurt cataracts,
> rending the hills ten miles away.
> Listen to the thunder;
> look, there is snow.

Scrupulous care, the felicitous arrangement of sound, and the repetition of "as if" *(nandŭt)* four times in the original enable the reader to experience nature's intricate and consummate artistry:

> Ah, extravagant celestial creator!
> What abundance of strange forms!
> Some fly, some dash—
> some stand, some soar—
> as if planting lotus,
> bundling white jade,
> sifting the Eastern Sea from its bed,
> and heaving up the North Pole!
> Lofty Height Viewing Terrace
> and lonely Cave Viewing Peak
> shoot into the blue
> and speak to the Maker
> from aeons
> constant and unbending.

On Buddha's Head Terrace:

> a cliff hanging in air
> over a thousand fathoms deep.
> The Milky Way
> unrolls its filaments
> showing the warp and woof
> of its hemp cloth.

At the Mirror Cove:

> Behind old pines rimming like hedges
> I scan a ten-mile-long beach
> like ironed and stretched white silk;
> the water is calm and clear,
> I can count the grains of sand.

The poem moves in time, space, with subtly alternating visual and auditory imagery.

> Who enraged
> the already angered whale?
> It blows and spews,
> how giddying its tumult!
> The silver mountain is leveled;
> it crashes in every direction.
> What a sight—snow falls
> in the boundless sky of the fifth month!

Chŏng combines topographical and didactic motifs to communicate much in little as, when in Ch'ŏrwŏn, contemplating the past and the violent reversals of fortune, he addresses "Magpies chattering / at the palace site of Kung Ye," the cruel overreacher who proclaimed the short-lived kingdom of Late Koguryŏ at the end of Silla but was murdered during his flight from the government army. Other examples of such succinctness include his punning on the name of the Korean town Hoeyang to refer to the Chinese town Huai-yang and his allusion to Chi Ch'ang-ju, a good official under the Emperor Wu of the Han. On seeing cranes nesting on Diamond Terrace, the speaker imagines that they greet Lin Pu, "master of the West Lake," the grower of plum trees and keeper of cranes. More pointed moral reflection occurs atop Vairocana Peak:

> Who said the kingdom of Lu
> was small?
> Who said all under heaven
> appeared to him [Confucius] small?
> Ah, how could we know
> its limits?
> Better descend,
> if you cannot gain the summit.

While counting twelve thousand peaks in clear air, the poet muses:

> If we could gather the air's vitality,
> pure yet clean,
> clean yet pure,

> on every peak
> and every crest
> and bring it back to create a man!

Here, as a victim of factional strife, he gives voice to his concern with major public issues. As a patient stoic lamenting the political disorder caused by small men, Chŏng indulges in an empty dream—if only we had great men at court! Evil courtiers blind the judgment of the ruler —hence his prayer, "May the clouds / never cover the sunlight," the sun standing for the king. Such evil, however, does not seem to threaten remote provinces such as Kangwŏn:

> flagpoles for filial sons
> adorn the valleys.
> Truly the people of Yao and Shun
> still seem to linger here.

Chŏng Ch'ŏl also draws on his native tradition, as when he muses on the whereabouts of four knights of Silla, who were thought to have tarried at the Three Days Cove, and recalls the romance of Hongjang, the despair of men of letters.

The poem ends on a festive note. Under the influence of "a cup of enchanting wine" (literally "Flowing Mist"), he, like Su Shih in his rhymeprose, "The Red Cliff, 2," is visited by an immortal who travels on a crane's back. Like Li Po, the poet is a banished immortal who can "stride into the great void." But when dream fades, "only a jade flute rings in the void." The speaker looks downward to discover the limitless sea illuminated by the moon. It shines not only on a thousand hills but on the myriad villages he is about to administer as a public servant.

Both the "Hymn of Constancy" *(Sa miin kok)* and the "Continued Hymn of Constancy" *(Sok miin kok)* are allegorical poems in the style of "Encountering Sorrow" *(Li sao)* and "The Nine Declarations" *(Chiu chang).*[32] They were written around 1585–1587 when the poet was forced by partisan strife to retire from court and spend several years in the countryside. In both poems he compares his loyalty to King Sŏnjo with that of a faithful wife longing for her absent husband or beloved. Poems on the theme of the neglected or forsaken wife are as old as the

Book of Songs. But in the Korean adaptations and imitations of "Encountering Sorrow" and "The Nine Declarations," especially "Thinking of a Fair One" *(Ssu mei-jen),* among the latter the unemployed or exiled courtier expresses his longing for the center of power in terms drawn from the vocabulary of love and derives his artistic detachment from parallels established between his frustrations and the rejected woman's disappointment in love. Decorum declares that the Fair One or Lovely One—the king—cannot be equated with a woman, especially in a society where woman's place was subordinate. Therefore, it is the speaker who has to assume the woman's persona. (One must not confuse this convention with the courtly love tradition in the West, where the lady is an agent of the courtier's spiritual development and is accorded power and fame by the poet.)

The first poem is a monologue by a fairy who is banished from the Moon Palace, literally the Great Cold Palace. It has six sections—introduction, the second, third, fourth, and fifth sections corresponding to the four seasons, and conclusion. Every season reminds her of her wretched state: plum blossoms and the dusky moon in spring; the making of warm clothes in summer; wild geese, the moon and stars, and snow in autumn; and tall bamboo at sunset, long night, cold quilt, and the harp in winter. Like all calendrical poems, the "Hymn of Constancy" combines similarity and contrasts, variety and continuity. Representing the stages of a woman's life, the four seasons seem to rush by, but there is no possibility for a liberation from the torments of love. Hence her desire for metamorphosis into a butterfly like the transformation of Alcyone and Ceyx into halcyons.[33]

> Better to die
> and become a butterfly,
> stop at each flower,
> rest upon each branch,
> with scented wings,
> and light upon his cloak.
> He may not remember me:
> yet I will follow him.

The "Continued Hymn of Constancy" is a dialogue between two fairies. The first starts out in search of her beloved in the hills and then by the river. Exhausted, she sinks into sleep and has a dream vision. But a frivolous rooster wakes her from her slumber. At the end, the first wishes to be a setting moon whereas the second wants to be a driving rain like the goddess of Mount Wu, who appeared to King Hsiang of Ch'u in the forms of clouds and rain.[34]

The epideictic strategy of the Korean country-house poems, such as Chŏng Ch'ŏl's "Little Odes on Mount Star" and Pak Illo's "Hall of Solitary Bliss," bear similarities to seventeenth-century English country-house poems—including the ideal landscape reflecting the virtue and character of the subject; the paradisiacal setting blessed with soil, air, wood, and water in Penshurst; an absence of display; idealization of the subject by associating him with paragons of virtue in the tradition; emblematic association of plants and animals with his virtue; and a combination of the topographical and the didactic. On the other hand, such Korean works omit any description of buildings or their pedigree, the role of the landed aristocracy in the rural community, tenants, retainers, and servants, communal life (public meals and gatherings), the subject's forefathers, and hyperbolic flattery with political implications. The epideictic poet's job is to create an enduring monument of poetry to stimulate emulation; hence the poem dwells on the subject's moral beauty and its lasting impact on society and culture. The praise of moral and spiritual excellence calls for a context of solitude and nature. Often explored are the dialectic patterns of withdrawal and emergence, the contemplative and the active, the self and the world: the contemplative as a necessary stage for an active career, moral cultivation as a prerequisite for public service, and the individual's moral sense as the only safeguard for institutions. Thus, in the course of describing the subject's moral beauty—be he a Taoist immortal or a Confucian sage—through praise of landscape, the poet reaffirms traditional cultural values and parades his knowledge of history and literature.

Written to praise the elegant life that Kim Sŏngwŏn (1525–1598) had established at the Mist Settling Hall and Resting Shadow Arbor on Mount Star in South Chŏlla province, Chŏng's "Little Odes on Mount Star" (*Sŏngsan pyŏlgok;* c. 1578) begins with a question:

> "Listen, Master of Mist Settling Hall
> and Resting Shadow Arbor,
> despite the many pleasures
> life held,
> why did you prefer to them all
> this mountain, this water?
> What made you choose
> the solitude of hills and streams?"

The poet then catalogues the delights of the four seasons and exclaims that Mount Star exceeds in beauty T'ao Ch'ien's Peach Blossom Spring;[35] it is, in fact, "the land of the immortals." This is a topos of outdoing, but it could also be a reflection of the patriotic theme. The expansive landscape reflects Kim Sŏngwŏn's own liberality, freedom, and unworldliness, and the floating clouds and waterfowl mentioned elsewhere in the poem symbolize the mind and courtesy of the host. Thus the poet is all the more cautious against the intrusion of cultural barbarians:

> Don't boast of
> the recluse's riches
> lest some find out
> this lustrous, hidden world.

The poet then meditates on heaven, man, and fortune in a lament for his own age and indeed all ages:

> Alone, deep in the mountains,
> with the classics, pile on pile,
> I think of the men
> of all times:
> many were sages,
> many were heroes.
> Heavenly intention goes
> into the making of men.
> Yet fortunes
> rise and fall;
> chance seems unknowable.
> And sadness deep.

At the end the poet, enraptured by the music played by his host on the black zither, claims that Kim is the true immortal in harmony with the workings of the universe, metaphorically flying high on the back of a crane. The crane is not only a symbol of longevity but a fitting emblem of unity and harmony. It soars above the world while maintaining an intimate relation with it, uniting time and space, time and timelessness.

Chŏng Ch'ŏl was a major writer of *sijo* as well. (Among the seventy-nine poems contained in his *Works,* poems 44, 45, 64, 70, and 77 are wrongly attributed to him.)[36] Unlike his *kasa* poems, in his *sijo* Chŏng drew much of his vocabulary from common words and phrases and found his inspiration in Korean sources. His *sijo* poems are simple in their syntax and diction, and he does not hesitate to use colloquial expressions, perhaps from a desire to provide the *sijo* with words from the native stock. Skilled in the admirable treatment of obvious themes, his poems are free from recondite figures of speech or obscure allusions. Like Pak Illo's "Songs of the Five Relations," the first seventeen poems, written to teach the people when he was governor of Kangwŏn province, demonstrate his fidelity to the cult of moral verse extant in the Chosŏn dynasty.

Chŏng's bitter resentment of court intrigue and the royal folly of which he was a victim provides his favorite theme. Following the tradition of "Encountering Sorrow," the poet still searches for his "lord," the king, despite the mistreatment he has suffered at his hands (poems 18, 19, 20, 23, 28, 29, 30, 32, 34, 71, 74, and 78). His longing to see his king finds expression in his desire for metamorphosis into, successively, a bird (poem 28), the rapids of the Han River that flows past the capital (poem 29), or the moon (poem 30) so that he may shine down upon the king to illuminate and rectify his heart. The speaker also sends a snow-covered pine bough, a sign of constancy, to his king. Poem 74 verges on hopelessness. Favors once granted are now withheld, the king is out of reach, and the speaker's memory and desire give way to pain. Poem 42 is a vigorous work that sternly warns the king not to be influenced by slander. In poem 48, an exercise in veiled vituperation, the movements of sycophants are compared to those of carpenters running about to no purpose with "ink cup and measure."[37] Flatterers and calumniators disrupt order and turn the structure into "a tumbledown shack." Small men are "carpenters" who ought to strengthen the royal edifice. The imagery of carpentry traces its pedigree to the Confucian tradition that the acceptance of honest admonition is a requisite of a good ruler. As wood is made straight by the use of a plumb line, so a ruler must be guided by the pattern of former kings. Broad learning and daily examination of his conduct are therefore often likened to the application of the plumb line, measure, square, and compass. Hence the poem's oblique censure of royal folly, and the misuse of royal authority that flowed downward to his ministers, culminating in the disastrous disunity that characterized the realm. The king's neglect of his roles untunes the string of harmony and foments factiousness at court. The "sick tree" (poem 44) on which no bird alights reinforces the message: denied the promise of life, the royal garden has become a bleak and desolate place.

Another group of poems is allegorical and compares the Old Man of the South Pole (poem 33) and the crane (poems 35 and 37) to the speaker's state of mind. The poet is like the polestar or the crane in the sky scorning the dusty world below. His ideal is to remain "unstained by the world" (poem 53):

> A dash of rain upon
> The lotus leaves. But the leaves
> Remain unmarked, no matter
> How hard the raindrops beat.
> Mind, be like the lotus leaves,
> Unstained by the world.

Therefore, he flings off his silk robe and dons the sedge cape and horsehair hat, the traditional garb of the recluse, declaring "I have nothing left that will stain me" (poem 76).

The third group of poems is autobiographical and deals with wine, the black zither, and the poet's life as a recluse. The poet's love of wine is well revealed in poems 21, 22, 24, 25, 26, 50, 54, 56, and 58, in which he exchanges imaginary questions and answers with wine. Poems 27, 31, 46, 59, and 63 also deal with wine. Poems 36 and 65 concern Chŏng's understanding of the technique of the black zither;[38] poems 57 and 75 demonstrate his skill in composing conventional love songs.

The meaning of four poems (nos. 60, 66, 67, 78) is indeterminate, mainly because of the ambiguity of the speaker's sex (the pronoun is omitted) and conventional imagery. The speaker who says "Would I change my first love, / My heart fresh as jade" (poem 60) could well be a man, a courtier who is protesting to the king his fidelity to his ideal love. The speaker in "My love is a thousand miles away; / I cannot sleep" (poem 66) and "But you send me no word— / How sad, my love!" (poem 67) could well be an abandoned woman lamenting her separation from her beloved. On the other hand, the speaker in "Autumn is almost gone; / He still keeps silent" (poem 78) could be either a man or a woman; in any case, the evening sun, cackling geese, burning maples, and feathery reeds prompt in the speaker a renewed desire for reunion. Similarly, the meaning of poem 51 is unclear:

> Let us strain sour wine and drink
> Until our mouths become sour.
> Let us steam bitter herbs and chew them
> Until they turn sweet.
> Let us walk around
> Until the nails in our clogs have worn flat.

Here the subject might be consistency, carrying something to perfection, or transforming misfortune into happiness.

PAK ILLO

Little is known of Pak Illo's formal education or his youth. The first definite date given in his biography is 1592, when he joined an army to fight Japanese invaders. Later the same year Pak was ordered to report for duty by Regional Commander of the Left Bank Sŏng Yunmun (fl. 1591–1607).[39] In 1599 he passed the military service examination and was appointed myriarch *(manho)* at Chorap'o, an isolated garrison on Kŏje Island, off the Korean coast.[40] In 1605 he was named a shipmaster of Pusan, and in the same year his military career ended.[41]

One day Pak was struck by a saying of Confucius—"In the morning, hear the Way; in the evening, die content" *(Analects,* 4.8)—and immediately resolved to master the Confucian classics and Neo-Con-

fucian philosophy. His learning was such, it is said, that the Duke of
Chou visited him in his dreams to deliver him from his ignorance.[42]
Thereafter he would burn incense at night and commune with the spirits of ancient sages. He drew diagrams illustrating the norms espoused
in the *Doctrine of the Mean,* the *Great Learning,* and the *Elementary
Learning,* and he meditated on them day and night.[43] In 1601 Pak met
the provincial official Yi Tŏkhyŏng for the first time. About 1619, Pak
visited Chang Hyŏngwang (1554–1637) and Cho Hoik (1545–1609) and
asked them for instruction. Pak wrote several poems in Chinese for
Chang, as well as twenty-nine *sijo* (nos. 7–35) describing the beauty of
Standing Rock (Ibam) in Yŏngil, where Chang had a retreat.[44] In 1619
Pak made friends with Chŏng Ku (1543–1620), a specialist in mathematics, military science, medicine, and geomancy. Pak visited Pepper
Well (Sukchŏng) in Ulsan together with Chŏng and wrote two *sijo*
(nos. 5–6) in which he compares Chŏng to Chu Hsi ("Master Chu").[45]
Comprising twenty-five poems, "Songs of the Five Relations" (nos.
36–60) assigns five poems each to the first four relations and two
poems to the last, with a conclusion of three. The last eight poems
were written around 1636.

   Pak's *sijo* poems are sternly, sometimes woodenly, didactic. Standing Rock, for example, inspires the speaker to muse on its firmness
and uprightness. Lofty and straight, it soars above the heavens (no.
20), touching the shining bodies in the great universe; it "bears him
up" (no. 18) and can purify his "base and cluttered mind." He likens it
to a "great hero" (no. 8) and to a man of virtue unrecognized and unrewarded (no. 9). In his dialogue with the rock, the speaker expresses
the wish that he too will "grow old together" with the rock (no. 15);
but it reminds him as well of the relativity of time, for the rock can
stand aeons but man cannot (no. 16). The arduous ascent to its summit is compared to the stages of self-cultivation (no. 11)—a determined
effort to advance in the Way. Hence he enjoins the reader to be careful
in his behavior "at a place unseen and unheard of" (no. 19)—he who
follows the Confucian Way must abide in reverence to interiorize
moral and spiritual cultivation. Pak then turns his gaze to the stream
and sees how it returns to the source "even when split into separate
streams" (no. 24). One may temporarily go astray, unable to control

his feelings, but in the end he returns to his "source" and commits himself to attainment of his goal. The speaker is also intent on outdoing his ancient exemplars, as the rock compares him to Yen Kuang (no. 14). But then, having preserved his equanimity and attained a sense of nondiscrimination, the speaker says he does not envy Tseng Hsi (no. 27) or Yen Kuang (no. 30). Having emulated the recluse farmers Ch'ang-chü and Chieh-ni, he can declare: "I have nothing to envy" (no. 31).

In "Songs of the Five Relations," the speaker avows that what distinguishes man from "birds and beasts" are the Five Relations (no. 58). Elsewhere Chŏng Ch'ŏl compared men without social virtue to "horses and oxen / Wearing caps and cowls and eating rice" (no. 8). Pak's series ends (no. 60) with an impassioned plea to his "juniors," probably his intended audience:

> My writing may be clumsy,
> But it is filled with sincerity and seriousness.
> Scan my poems and savor them;
> Then you will need no other aid.

Pak may have been intent on acquiring learning and virtue, but he did not fully understand how to make his poetry ethical. He might have thought himself a custodian of morality; but his marked sententiousness, strings of authorities (the Confucian canon), and exempla—homiletic and pedagogic zeal gone awry—sometimes make him appear little more than a mouthpiece for Confucian ideology. There are no violent attacks on his *sijo* nor any warm tributes to them—perhaps because of his undistinguished pedigree as a commoner.

When, on 24 May 1592, at the time of the Monkey (3–5 P.M.), the Japanese army landed at the Korean port of Pusan, official relations between the two countries were already suspended because of Japanese pirates' raids and Korea's refusal to permit the Japanese warlord Toyotomi Hideyoshi's intended invasion of Ming China through Korea. Totally unprepared for the attack, Korea suffered a crushing defeat from the beginning, owing also to factional struggles and divided opinions at court. As the invasion forces marched to Seoul, King Sŏnjo fled the capital for the north (9 June). The Japanese occupied Seoul (14 June) and then P'yŏngyang (14 July). With the help of the Ming army, however, P'yŏngyang was retaken in February 1593 and the king and his court returned to Seoul in October of the same year. Under Admiral Yi Sunsin (1545–1598), the Korean navy defeated the Japanese fleets in sea battle after sea battle—from the first engagement at Jade Cove (Okp'o; 16 June 1592) to the last at Dew Ferry (Noryang; 16 December 1598) when the admiral died in action. The poet Pak Illo was no doubt proud of having been a member of the Korean navy that had established command of the sea. The subject of Pak's first *kasa* is based on his experience in late 1598.[46]

The "Song of Peace" *(T'aep'yŏng sa)* was written at the time of Japanese withdrawal from Korea to encourage the soldiers under his command by predicting the advent of a peaceful era. The poem's five sections concern the sudden onslaught of the Japanese army and the king's escape; the recapture of P'yŏngyang by the Ming army and ensuing negotiations between China and Japan; another battle; and a return to the barracks and celebration of victory. These are followed by the poet's statement of his resolve to be loyal and filial and brighten the Five Relations and, finally, a prayer to heaven which summarizes his recurrent concerns:

> So we pray that you bless our dynasty;
> that the royal house be endless;
> that the sun and moon of the Three Dynasties
> shine on the golden age of Yao and Shun;
> that there be no more war
> for myriad years;
> that people till the field and dig wells
> and sing the praises of peace;
> that we always have a holy king above us;
> and that he and we share the joy of peace.

The year 1605 brought further signs of Japanese movement off the southeastern coast, and Pak was named a shipmaster in Pusan. On this occasion he composed "Lament on the Water" *(Sŏnsang t'an)*. After an introduction, the poem discusses the origin of ships. The speaker blames the Yellow Emperor for having invented the ship and the First Emperor of the Ch'in for having dispatched Hsü Shih, or Hsü Fu, with a company of boys and girls to remote islands to obtain the pills of immortality. He argues that descendants of those boys and girls settled on Japanese islands and became ancestors of the Japanese people. But then the poet reconsiders and admits that, without a ship or boat, a recluse like Chang Han could not have indulged in his noble pursuits south of the river and a fisherman could not "enjoy his life free as duckweed, / a life better than that of three dukes, / among matchless hills and waters." He then notes the difference between such boats and his own ship:

> In olden days
> wine tables crowded ships;
> today,
> only large swords and long spears.
> A ship it is,
> but not as ships once were.

He then vows to repulse the enemy and hopes for their imminent surrender, for only then can he "sing in a fishing boat / in autumn moon and spring breeze, / and laying our heads on high pillows, / we'll see once more the happy era / when all the waters sing in unison."

Following Confucian historiographic convention, Pak chooses words with dark, damning connotations. The Japanese invaders are "island savages and barbarians" *(toi),* "wicked bandits" *(kunhyung),* "a horde of outlaws" *(chŏkto),* "wily outlaws" *(hwalchŏk),* "unruly outlaws" *(nandangjŏk),* "thieves of mice and dogs" *(sŏjŏl kut'u),* and "wriggling island savages" *(chunp'i toi).* He also speaks of "crafty designs of pirates" *(haech'u hyungmo)* and relegates them to the status of animals, as in "lairs for wolves and foxes" *(sit'ogul).* These terms all appear in Chinese graphs. The technical term *i,* as in "Eastern Barbarians," is the word used by Chinese historians to designate the Japanese and Koreans. *Ku (k'ou)* means "to plunder" as a verb and "bandits, thieves, raiders" as a noun; *hyung (hsiung),* "bad, unlucky"; *chŏk (ts'e),* "a thief, rebel, an outlaw." To brand one's enemy in this fashion is a customary practice everywhere. To paint them in the darkest hue as destroyers of society and civilization, without valor and virtue, is in the convention of "praise and blame" as old as the Confucian classics.

In the autumn of 1601, Yi Tŏkhyŏng (1561–1613) arrived in Yŏngch'ŏn as inspector of provincial administration and met Pak for the first time. Pak composed four *sijo* poems (nos. 1–4) for Yi in return for the latter's gift of a basketful of persimmons. In 1611, Yi was forced to leave the court due to party strife and retired to Dragon Ford to spend his last years. Pak used to visit him there, whereupon the host would unburden his heart to the poet. Yi knew of Pak's ability and moral courage, and intended to recommend him, but the exile died in 1613 at the age of fifty-two before he could do so. The "Song of the Sedge Bank" *(Saje kok)* describes scenic spots at Sedge Bank and the idle life and elegant pleasures that Yi enjoyed there. Although a note accompanying the poem says that Pak wrote this poem for Yi, it appears that Pak incorporated details from his own biography when he mentions his own mother: "[I will] invite my mother, thus fulfilling / a son's duty till the last." In fact, the poem ends with the poet's determination to serve his ailing mother:

> . . . I'll serve her and age with her
> with the cleansed ears of Hsü Yu,
> with the costumes of Lao Lai Tzu,
> until the pines have turned to green iron,
> the pines thick in the stream out front.

Asked by Yi Tŏkhyŏng about his life in the mountains, Pak wrote his most famous *kasa:* "In Praise of Poverty" *(Nuhang sa)*. The title itself, literally "Song of the Mean Lane," was inspired by a passage in the *Analects* (6.9) where master praises his disciple Yen Hui: "Incomparable indeed was Hui! A handful of rice to eat, a gourdful of water to drink, living on a mean street."[47] The poem begins with an admission of the speaker's impracticality and clumsiness (cooking gruel with wet straw), but the tone is self-satirical in view of a passage in the *Lao Tzu* (45): "The greatest skill is like clumsiness." Strategically placed at the center of the poem is a lament on his need for a farmhand, as well as an ox, without which there can be no plowing. Then comes a wry, humorous episode in which he makes futile efforts to borrow an ox from a rich farmer who was bribed by a peasant with wine. After a sleepless night and a disappointing morning, the speaker resolves to forgo plowing and instead contemplates the green bamboo in the winding waters of the Ch'i, an allusion to poem 55 in the *Book of Songs*. He then invokes "the flowery reeds" and "the unsold breeze and unsold moon," intensely polemical symbols, as we shall soon see. Then comes another allusion to a quotation from the *Analects* (14.11), "To be poor and not resent it is far harder than to be rich yet not presumptuous,"[48] followed by a panegyric to the modest life. The last lines emphasize that poverty cannot bend the noble mind. His only concern is how to delight in the pursuit of the Confucian way:

> A handful of rice and a gourdful of water
> are enough for me.
> To be well fed and well clad
> is not my dream.
> In this world, peaceful and quiet,
> let's be loyal and filial,
> harmonious with brothers, faithful to friends.
> Such a life allows no reproof.
> As for other matters,
> let them come as they will.

Throughout his poetry Pak Illo emphasizes by constant reference to the classics the importance of the acquisition of knowledge in the Confucian tradition. The overall pattern therefore indicates the interplay of the formal and the informal, the sophisticated and the rustic, the learned and the personal, the *utile* and *dulce,* as the poet seeks to adopt moderation in life and art. Thus with humor, irony, anecdote, conversation, and a bit of self-satire, Pak has created a convincing picture of a poor but noble poet-farmer's life.

Pak's "Hall of Solitary Bliss" was written on the occasion of his poetic pilgrimage to the Hall of Solitary Bliss on Mount Purple Jade in Kyŏngju, where the remains of Yi Ŏnjŏk (1491–1553) are preserved and Pak paid tribute to the master's memory. Yi Ŏnjŏk passed the civil service examination in 1514 and served as Fourth Inspector and Second Censor before he suffered in the 1530 purge and withdrew to Mount Purple Jade near Kyŏngju to study Neo-Confucian philosophy. In 1537 he was recalled by royal order and filled the following posts: Rector of the National Academy, Inspector-General, Minister of Personnel,

Rites, and Punishments, Magistrate of Seoul, First Counselor in the Office of Special Counselors, and Fourth State Counselor (1545). The "Hall of Solitary Bliss" does not dwell on his political achievements, however, but on his exemplary virtues. The poet's task is to exalt and perpetuate virtue. Describing the ideal Confucian statesman and philosopher, Pak writes:

> He revered the sages of the past
> and wrote poems.
> In peaceful nature he was so immersed
> that he felt at home in all situations.
> . . . .
> He contemplated, sought truth,
> cultivated learning and virtue.

Pak goes on to say that through study and self-cultivation, Yi preserved and continued tradition and "opened a bright new path."

> His thousand words and myriad sayings
> are all wisdom, each revealing
> a long tradition and ways of thought
> as bright as the sun and moon—
> light
> illuminating the dark.

As a statesman he was equal to Hou Chi or Lord Millet, ancestor of the Chou dynasty, and Chieh, a wise minister under the legendary Emperor Shun. But caught in a political purge of 1547, he was sent into exile to the north where, like the Grand Tutor Chia I (201–168 B.C.) in Ch'ang-sha,[49] he spent seven years in cold Kanggye. There he transformed the rigors of the political winter into the bliss of a virtuous spring.

The poem utilizes such metaphors of natural harmony as graceful mountain peaks, a winding stream, straight bamboo, a caressing wind, and a dense pine grove and implies that these were spared by heaven and treasured by earth so that their riches could be handed down to the true "owner." The emphasis is on the beauty, purity, and spontaneity of nature, symbolic of the subject's harmonious, enlightened state of mind. The hall itself is a center of moral cultivation;

what is praised is a way of life in the ideal setting, a mode of existence vital to the preservation of the enduring norms of the lettered class. Friends there are said to include such emblematic animals as hawks and fishes. These classical images from poem 239 in the *Book of Songs*[50] imply the self-contentedness of even birds and fish as first, as in the original context, a sign of the extent of moral transformation effected by an ideal ruler (though here fish do not jump into the fishermen's nets in their eagerness to serve the owner)[51] and, second, as emblems of the workings of the Confucian Way—how it is clearly seen in heaven and on earth.

Yi's retreat surpasses in beauty and purity the Garden of Solitary Bliss of Ssu-ma Kuang (1019–1086), Censer Peak on Mount Lu, sung of by Li Po, the T'ient'ai Mountains in Chekiang, or even Peach Blossom Spring, the Chinese Arcadia. When its master is absent, the hall is like an empty hill without a phoenix, yet his fragrance lingers on, for the speaker sees him "in the soup and on the walls." In moral and spiritual stature Yi Ŏnjŏk is compared to Mount T'ai or the polestar, supreme emblems of Confucian moral rhetoric. Such hyperbolic description and metonymical representation create the *locus amoenus* —an ideal microcosm that mirrors the ideal state built on the Confucian political-moral philosophy. But on another level—since in Confucianism the disrupter of social and moral harmony is man himself— the poet has subtly introduced a satirical bite. That is, the images of perfection and hyperbolic praise indirectly deride those ignorant of the ideal pattern of emergence and withdrawal, the art of biding time, and cultivation of the self. A victim of political machination and senseless bloodshed which upset the moral and cosmic harmony, Yi's dream of creating another golden age was shattered and the country became a wasteland. Still, even in exile he "cultivated virtue, the forthright Way," and history eventually vindicated his name, private academies enshrined him, and he was worshipped in the Confucian Temple, the highest honor accorded a scholar-statesman. Thus he was able to make use of adversity as a trial of spirit. "Jade is concealed in the rock, yet the hill is refulgent with it,[52] says a passage in Lu Chi's *Essay on Literature* aptly evoked to exalt the master's rural solitude, contemplative leisure, and complete modesty.

Virtue therefore serves as a bulwark against mutability. The man who dwells in the Hall of Solitary Bliss has conquered time by his paradigmatic acts, and his enduring virtues are bright as the sun and moon, eternal as the cool wind that blows through the hall itself.

> Heaven so high and earth so rich,
> they, too, will dissolve into dust.
> None is eternal but the cool wind that blows
> through the Hall of Solitary Bliss.

"Only the perennial fragrance of my teacher abides," the poet declares. Virtue, not fame, conquers death. Yi Ŏnjŏk thus becomes an ideal. Side by side the poet sets down the perennial contrastive values and norms of conduct: Confucian and Taoist, world and self, man and nature. The poet, however, affirms these values of history and culture which insist on the correspondence between microcosm and macrocosm, society and nature. Subtly underlying the poem is the poet's conviction that the return of political-moral harmony depends upon the return of harmony between man and nature. The restoration of civil order calls for man's moral regeneration, but action might bring about a faster change hastening the application of the Arcadian vision to the world of politics. Such a dream, combining the active and the contemplative, finds expression in the country-house poems. As a man's dwelling expresses his virtue, so should a dynasty. The implication is that only a ruler's bestowal of virtue on people and country can transform chaos into order and reaffirm the values of civilization. The ideal landscape, then, provides a setting in which to contemplate the enduring norms of history and culture.

The "Song of the Southeast" (*Yŏngnam ka;* 1635) is another praise poem, written when Yi Künwŏn, governor of the south, was about to resign his position in 1635. Moved by his good administration, the people asked him to remain in office. As a model public servant, Yi took "seventy districts as a family,"

> and with a mother or father's heart,
> looking upon motherless people
> as infants,

he bestowed love
sweet as raindrops over the grain crops
in the time of drought,
fresh as water in a pool
to a fish in a dry rut.

Yi ruled not by law and decree but by personal example: he encouraged agricultural and sericultural production, military preparation, and education. ("Teaching human relations at school / was the basis of his rule / that serves the Way of Master K'ung.") County magistrates emulate his pattern, thus creating an ideal agricultural community in which, as in the days of the sage-emperor Shun, there is no longer litigation. The poem concludes with the speaker's suggestion for hero worship:

Let's buy white silk
and bright colors,
paint his portrait in full figure,
and hang it on the walls
of every house in the southeast,
and when his face flashes through our mind,
we'll see our beloved minister.

Pak wrote his last *kasa*, "Song of the Reedy Stream" *(Nogye ka)*, in the spring of 1636, seven years before his death. Reedy Stream is in a valley near Taehyŏn village, Sannae town *(myŏn)*, in Wŏlsŏng county *(kun)*, where the poet built himself a grass roof, "leaning on a huge rock" and "fronting the stream with the hills behind." Birds and beasts are his cattle, and he fishes under the moon or plows the "fields among the clouds." His one worry is how to provide for his children:

I can divide among my children
endless hills and waters and idle fields.
But I fear it's hard to allot
a bright moon and clear breeze.
I'd rather choose him who serves my will,
be he gifted or not,
and leave him all
in a certificate drawn by Li Po and T'ao Ch'ien.

> You say my words
> are ignorant of the world;
> but what else have I
> for my children but these?

Even when he tries to fish, he cannot bring himself to "drop a line to deceive" the fishes who know him, although later he does indulge in an imaginary feast of viands and dainties (luscious bracken, scented angelica, pork, venison, fresh-minced perch, *nul* fish, and pheasant). He believes he owes his leisurely life-style to royal favor and ends the poem with a prayer:

> May my holy king enjoy long life
> until every hill is made low and every sea runs dry.
> In the bright, contented world,
> let the sun and moon shine on a peaceful reign,
> let swords be sheathed
> for a thousand and myriad years,
> that people might sing of the blessings of peace
> when they work the fields or dig wells,
> that this body among hills and waters
> might like the winds and moon never age.

In summary, Pak's first concern was with the Five Relations— between ruler and minister, father and son, husband and wife, elder and younger brothers, and friends. Filial piety, as we have noted, is often extolled. Pak's respect and love for his teacher, who embodies Confucian virtues, is fondly dealt with in the "Song of the Sedge Bank" and "The Hall of Solitary Bliss." In the latter poem, the language glows with personal admiration for this teacher, whose absence is betokened by the image of "an empty hill without a phoenix." Of all the Five Relations, Pak's loyalty to his king is especially evident in all his poems. In times of national crisis the speaker, "imbued with public spirit, / with knapsacks and bags / full of small provisions," takes to the field "to die in the last ditch." In times of peace he regrets his absence from the court and prays for the king:

> When I raise my head
> toward the polestar,

secret tears
often wet my sleeves.   ("Song of the Sedge Bank")

However incapable,
I am your subject.
The way of success being different today,
I have grown old without serving at your side.   ("Lament on the Water")

Often I raise my eyes
to the polestar,
shedding secret tears
in a corner of the sky.   ("Song of the Reedy Stream")

Following the *Analects* (2.1), the king is likened to the polestar "which remains in its place while all the lesser stars do homage to it."[53] The ruler can be compared to a polestar, however, only if he rules by moral power. Examples of such ideal rulers are the legendary sage-emperors and the great ancestors of the ruling houses of the Shang and Chou. Pak's poems are peopled by such cultural heroes, sage-emperors, and wise ministers of the golden age as Fu Hsi, I Yin, Yao, Shun, Hou Chi, Kao Yao, Wu-huai, and Ko-t'ien, whose names he reveres.

Indeed, says Pak, one can become a virtuous and wise gentleman through learning—especially through the teachings of Confucius and the Neo-Confucian philosophers. Emphasis on the importance of knowledge in the Confucian tradition, as well as on culture, is supplied indirectly by constant references to and quotations from the Confucian canon. All are made to yield arguments in support of the poet's convictions. However, Sung philosophers such as Chou Tun-i (1017–1073), Ch'eng I (1033–1107), and Chu Hsi (1130–1200) are generally presented as learned recluses in a serene natural setting, while the places associated with them are used in similes and metonymies. The poet cannot see Korea's mountains and rivers without seeing the I or Lien rivers and the Wu-i or Tzu-yang mountains at the same time:

The emerald waves are wide and deep—
are they not the I and the Wei?   ("Song of the Sedge Bank")

Like the Wu-i Mountains,
the peaks look graceful,

and the river winds
like the I.   ("The Hall of Solitary Bliss")

But if the Way does not prevail, if virtuous men are neglected or slandered, if there is no place for integrity and justice, then it is best to "withdraw from one's generation" (*Analects,* 14.39). Pak therefore sought the calm and quiet of nature rather than the gilded titles of "three dukes." Another virtuous courtier might have done so with the thought that there was no place for him in the world; Pak, however, was seeking the seclusion that would enable him to cultivate his poetry. Therefore he became a recluse, a priest of the natural rituals. His life was patterned after the Way of nature, and nature with its manifold faces and endless mysteries became the object of his studies. Hence Hsü Yu, Ch'ao-fu, Ch'ang-chü, Chieh-ni, Chang Han, and Yen Kuang became his guardians, the paragons he held up in contrast to avaricious courtiers.

This contrast is subtly achieved by the use of a key adjective in Pak's poetry, perhaps the most ideological adjective that recurs in the *kasa* poetry of the Chosŏn dynasty. It is the verb *kabŏpta* in its adjectival form, *kabŏmnŭn,* and its cognate *nimjaeŏpta,* with its adjectival form *nimjaeŏpsan* and adverbial form *nimjaeŏpsi. Kabŏpta* has two meanings: (1) not worth putting a price on, having no value, hence not yet sold, and (2) having a value beyond all price. Pak Illo writes in the "Song of the Sedge Bank":

> Gulls and herons wheeling everywhere,
> numberless stags and hinds,
> these are the cattle
> that *I* raise here;
> and the unsold breeze and unsold moon,
> they too naturally belong to me.

"In Praise of Poverty" offers the lines:

> Among the flowery reeds,
> befriending the moon and the fresh breeze,
> I'll grow old naturally
> among the unsold breeze and unsold moon.

Again in the "Song of the Reedy Stream":

> Natural the silent green hills and waters,
> natural the bright moon and clear breeze;
> natural the unsold gulls and herons,
> natural, too, many stags and hinds.
> The field plowed by Ch'ang-chü and Chieh-ni,
> the fishing beach haunted by Yen Kuang,
> still unsold, natural, natural!

Nimjae ŏmnŭn, which is logically related to *kabŏmnŭn,* means "ownerless, as yet unclaimed" (sometimes "without a host"):

> I visit at just the right moment
> the Valley of the Reedy Stream.
> Peerless hills and waters
> have no owner, unattended . . .   ("Song of the Reedy Stream")

> Abandoned,
> unsurpassed nature is without a host . . .   ("Song of the Sedge Bank")

Indeed, sycophants at court, for all their power and wealth, could never buy, sell, or become part of the priceless nature that can be won only by the poet's sensibility and imagination. Corrupt courtiers have rank and riches; but only the poet can find joy in nature. This love of priceless nature, whose significance is comprehended only by the poet who has renounced the world, was the sine qua non of poetic existence. Hence another favorite expression among Chosŏn dynasty poets: I will not exchange these hills and waters for the titles of three dukes.

Although this life "free as duckweed" is in material terms a poor life, the poet declares that he is not resentful (*Analects,* 14.11). To him "any thought of accepting wealth and rank by means that he knows to be wrong is as remote from him as the clouds that float above" (*Analects,* 7.15).[54] Emphasis is therefore placed on his refusal to accept the spoils of corruption and his ability to remain content with what he has:

> Not enough, you say;
> but I never starve.
> How delicious is
> my corn in my hut!   ("Song of the Sedge Bank")

Poverty is no cause for concern to the noble mind, which seeks only to delight in the pursuit of the Way. In this connection, a word should be said about a quotation from the *Analects* (11.25) that appears repeatedly in Pak's, and all Chosŏn-dynasty, *kasa* poetry. While Tzu-lu, Jan Ch'iu, and Kung-hsi Hua desired power and political involvement, Tseng Hsi, in one of the most beautiful and Taoistic passages in the *Analects,* explains that he desires not a kingdom but a life in harmony with the *li,* with his fellow men, and with nature. Indeed, he was concerned with developing and refining this faculty in himself in order to become "a man among men." To such a man a lofty title is as meaningless as "floating clouds."

Pak lived in a society that hewed rigidly to Confucian morality and allowed expression of Confucian values by means of poetic devices. He drew heavily upon Chinese sources, it is true, and his works are derivative. Yet it was precisely such art that met the taste of the day with its stress on sophistication, erudition, occasional eloquence, and perfection of detail. Frequent resort to allusion, then, was not denounced in his day. Rather, it served to establish a community of mind, of imagination, and of life between the poet and his reader. Pak lived in the Taoist fashion, but he kept his spirit ever Confucian. The phrase that best summarizes his views on poetry is: "Poetry expresses in words the intent of the heart."[55]

YUN SŎNDO

Yun Sŏndo was the most accomplished poet writing in the *sijo* form. His lyrics are diverse in mood and technique, and his diction is peerless. Graceful, delicately varied rhythms are natural to him, and his every poem exhibits new techniques and a fresh tone. Yet his invention is so subtle that it becomes noticeable only after repeated close readings of his poems.

The first group of six poems, entitled "Dispelling Gloom" (*Kyŏnhoe yo,* 1618), are the earliest known poems by Yun. Although they tend to abstraction and a use of the pathetic fallacy, these poems sing with an intensity of their own and anticipate Yun's later poetic genius. In poem 4, for example, suspense is created by an emphatic repetition of verbs:

Moehŭn kilgo kilgo	A chain of mountains is long, long;
murŭn mŏlgo mŏlgo	Waters flow far, far.
ŏbŏi kŭrinttŭdŭn	Love for parents is endless,
mank'o mank'o hago hago	And my heart is heavy.
ŏdŭisyŏ woegirŏginŭn	Faroff, crying sadly,
ulgo ulgo kanŭni.	A lone wild goose flies by.

The five adjectival verbs in the conjunctive form *ko* are among the simplest of Korean verbs, but tension builds as the poem moves steadily from one verb in the *ko* form to the next.[56] The long vowels in *kilgo, mŏlgo,* and *mank'o* and the *l*'s in *kil, mŏl,* and *ul* provide a resonant, stately note. In poem 6 Yun employs a rhetorical question for emphasis and dramatic contrast:

Kujŭnbi kaedan malka	Has the dreary rain ceased?
hŭridŏn kurŭm kŏttan malka	Have the dark clouds rolled away?

Yun was told of a certain court minister who repented and mended his failings while in exile at Kyŏngwŏn. At that very moment the dreary rain ceased and the clouds rolled away. The poet wrote these lines to console himself. Here the "dreary rain" and the "dark clouds" are closely bound up with the poet's attitude toward corrupt officials and his political enemies. The "deep swamps" in the poem subtly enhance the poem's mood and contrast two different states of affairs. The muddy swamps, possibly a metaphor for the quagmire of court life, become a "limpid" place where the poet can wash his cap strings, alluding to the example of Ch'ü Yüan. Similar rhetorical questions appear in poem 28, as well as in a sequence of four didactic poems.

In the group of poems entitled "New Songs in the Mountain," Yun's masterpiece is the "Songs of Five Friends" *(Ou ka),* written in praise of water, stone, pine, bamboo, and the moon. By naming five natural objects as his friends, rather than his fickle fellow men, the poet has won a new domain for himself and his poetry. Indeed, he has established a relationship with nature that is the reserve of those possessing poetic sensibility. In poem 20 tension is achieved by developing the theme with successive contrasts through the fifth line. The tension is resolved only in the sixth line, at the very end of the poem:

Kurŭm pitch'i chot'ahana	They say the color of clouds is fine,
kŏmkirŭl charo handa.	But they often darken.
Paramsorae maktahana	They say the sound of winds is clear,
kŭch'il chŏgi hanomaera.	But they often cease to blow.
Chok'odo kŭch'il nwi ŏpkinŭn	It is only *water,* then,
mul ppunin'ga hanora.	That is perpetual and good.

The effect is achieved by a skillful use of the simple adversative particle *hana* (translated as "but") in the first and third lines with the reply given immediately following, in the second and fourth lines respectively. The adjectives describing "color of clouds" and "sound of winds" are extremely simple, yet they are at once concise and clear and natural. Even more important, they were chosen specifically because their sounds enhance the rhythmic flow of the poem as a whole. In poem 23 Yun introduces yet another device:

Namodo anin kŏsi	You are not a tree,
p'uldo anin kŏsi . . .	Nor are you a plant.

First, the omission of the conjunction *ko* between the first and second lines produces a unique intonation and rhythm that quicken the movement of the lines. Second, the ending -*i* in this context normally anticipates the interrogative adverb *ŏtchi* or *ŏi*. ("You are not a tree; but *why* . . .?") *Ŏi* appears only in the fourth line, however, keeping the reader in suspense and heightening the poem's dramatic effect. The poem moves rapidly through this construction by repetition of *anin* in the first and second lines and the appearance of *nwi* ("who") in the third. Furthermore, in the original the poem never specifically mentions the bamboo to which it is addressed, but only its characteristics. Thus the six lines comprising the poem rush on like a waterfall, keeping the reader's mind ever on the alert.

"At the Beginning of the Feast" *(Ch'oyŏn kok)* and "At the End of the Feast" *(P'ayŏn kok;* nos. 29–32) are admonitions to the king, though it is uncertain whether they are in fact impromptu poems actually composed at a feast. In poem 29 "house" alludes to the ideal state, while "straight wood" denotes the benevolent government and moral power of the king. "Straight" in the third line also alludes to the ways of the ancient sage-kings. In poem 30, "wine" and "broth" allude to the virtues of the king, while "yeast," "salt," and "prunes" denote the wise ministers who assist in state affairs. Poem 31 urges moderation in the pursuit of pleasure. Perhaps the poet had in mind poem 114 in the *Book of Songs,* in the first stanza of which the monitor says, "Do not be so riotous / As to forget your home. / Amuse yourselves, but no wildness! / Good men are always on their guard."[57]

The image of the fisherman occurs from time to time in both East Asian and Western poetry, but nowhere does it play such an important role as in Korean poetry, particularly in the works of Yun Sŏndo. There the fisherman symbolizes a pure and wise figure who lives aloof from the woes of the day, scorns worldly ambition and personal glory, and devotes himself to cultivation of his sensibility and his self. Yun took his inspiration partly from traditional songs, but what he made of them is so original that we must give full credit to his masterful control of his materials and superior technique.

The origin of the *Ŏbu sa* (or *ka),* or "Angler's Songs," is obscure. Fishermen's songs were popular from the Koryŏ dynasty.[58] The earliest reference occurs in a heptasyllabic quatrain, "In Memory of Minister Kim Yŏngdon,"[59] in the *Ikchae chip,* 4.8b. A note immediately following the poem adds that Minister Kim ordered the female entertainer *(kisaeng)* P'yop'i to sing the angler's songs every time he drank wine. The first reference in Chosŏn dynasty annals occurs in the *T'aejong sillok,* 23.42a. At the banquet held in the Kyŏnghoe Tower in 1412, the former king (Chŏngjong) requested the skilled singer Kim Chasun to sing the angler's songs. Kim's performance so moved Chŏngjong that he rewarded the artist with fine garments. The author or compiler of the original twelve songs is unknown, but the popularity of the poems during the fifteenth and sixteenth centuries is attested by Yi Hwang (1501–1571), who provides the following information: At the banquet given by his uncle Yi U an old *kisaeng* from Andong sang the 'Angler's Songs' so well that he was delighted and jotted them down. . . . During his stay at court he often inquired whether anyone knew these songs, but nobody seemed to have the faintest idea. By chance he came across an anthology compiled by Pak Chun *(Akchang kasa)* that contains the texts of the poems. Hwang Chullyang (1517–1563)[60] copied them and presented them, together with the texts of ten shorter poems, to Yi Hyŏnbo (1467–1555).[61] Yi Hyŏnbo in turn recompiled the twelve songs into a cycle of nine[62] and the ten shorter poems into a cycle of five.[63] Our source further comments that upon obtaining the texts of the poems, Yi Hyŏnbo devoted himself to their revision and adaptation. The correspondence between Yi Hyŏnbo and Yi Hwang suggests that the former was careful in his work and submitted his drafts to the latter for comment at various points.

Although Yi Hyŏnbo did away with repetitions and reorganized the envoi (Korean nautical verbs), his adaptations with their faulty rhythms, heavy Chinese diction, and disunited tone still sound clumsy. In short, they have not yet been made into Korean poetry. The music of Korean, its intrinsic rhythm, is lacking. Indeed, Yun Sŏndo commented that "Yi's sound pattern is faulty, and his diction and meaning leave much to be desired." Yun therefore set out to create a cycle of angler's songs in the Korean vernacular that would resound with native rhythms. His forty poems, titled "The Angler's Calendar," depicting the four seasons are products of his leisurely life at a favorite retreat, the Lotus Grotto. They are written in intricate stanzas differing from the conventional *sijo* form. The general pattern is as follows (the numerals indicating the number of syllables in each metric segment):

1st line:	3	4	3	4
envoi:	4	4		
2nd line:	3	4	3	4
envoi:	3	3	3	
3rd line:	3	4	3	4

Thus a pair of four-syllable words is added after the first line, and three-syllable onomatopoetic words after the second line, thus bringing the total number of syllables to fifty-nine. The fortieth poem in this series has an unusual form, for here the total number of syllables is seventy-two.

The verbs in the ten first envois of each seasonal set of poems are not only well arranged in narrative sequence, but are identical from season to season: (1) cast off; (2) hoist anchor; (3) raise sail; (4) row away; (5) row away; (6) lower sail; (7) stop the boat; (8) moor the boat; (9) drop anchor; and (10) bring the boat ashore. Together with the intricate organization, the poems are marked by flawless use of the language and a musical quality that depicts images as well as simulating sounds. Indeed, Yun succeeded in casting an authentic depiction of the fisherman's life into lyrical rhythms.

The fourth poem in the spring cycle offers an admirable example of the poet's technique:

Unŭn kŏsi pŏkkugiga	Is it a cuckoo that cries?
p'urŭn kŏsi pŏdŭlsupka	Is it the willow that is blue?
iŏra iŏra	Row away, row away!
ŏch'on tuŏ chibi	Several roofs in a far fishing village
naesoge naraktŭrak . . .	Swim in the mist . . .

The poem opens with two questions suggesting uncertainty regarding the senses of sound and sight. In the next two lines we actually do see village roofs, however insubstantial they may appear, as they seem to swim in the twilight. The expression *naraktŭrak* suggests that the vision is splendid, even if tinged with unreality. The last two lines are brisk and forceful and express a practical and immediate concern with nature. In consequence we proceed from a state of near-illusion to one of magnificence dimly perceived and then to one of immediate appreciation and delight, with the suggestion that all these stages follow in sequence. The poem therefore presents nature's mystery, beauty, and bounty in terms of illusory loveliness, actual loveliness, and finally the physical sustenance reaped by those who fish. Thus the poem not only imparts the felt transcendence of the vision but reveals as well an awareness of the transience of earthly joy and beauty. Yet all this is conveyed with the simplest vocabulary and the utmost economy.

Yun Sŏndo was summoned to the capital by King Hyojong in 1652, but the poet's political enemies defamed and reviled him and within a month he retired to his retreat. There Yun wrote "The Disappointing Journey" (nos. 73–75; 1652), in which the "Jade Emperor" is King Hyojong himself and the "host of spirits" represents the poet's opponents. In the closing poem Yun laments the absence of wise ministers who could raise up the "White Jade Tower" by delivering the state from the evils of the day.

THREE MASTERS OF *SIJO* AND *KASA*

Committed to the vernacular genres of Korean poetry, Chŏng Ch'ŏl, Pak Illo, and Yun Sŏndo evince a mastery of generic conventions of the *sijo* and *kasa*. Fully recognizing the tradition's historicity, they knew how to create poetry from culture. But as poets writing at a particular point in Korean history, they also invest their work with current ideological themes: the importance of morality in the fashioning of the Confucian gentleman and social cohesion; alternative modes of existence (engagement versus withdrawal, court versus country, conformity versus naturalness, reason versus intuition); and the correspondence between microcosm and macrocosm. As products of the period in Korean history most strongly influenced by Neo-Confucianism, their topics reflect the perennial concerns of the literature of that time. My introduction has emphasized poetic codes and cultural norms of the age. The modifications these three poets brought to the generic conventions profoundly influenced later writers. That is why their works are still read and studied today.

Chŏng Ch'ŏl

1537	Born in Seoul as the eldest son of Chŏng Yuhang (17 January)
1551	Moves with his father to Ch'angp'yŏng, Chŏlla; studies with Kim Inhu (1510–1560) and others; marries a daughter of Yu Kanghang (four sons and two daughters)
1561	Obtains the "Literary Licentiate" degree
1562	Places first in another examination; appointed Fourth Inspector
1567	Chosen for the Lake Hall of Scholars; begins writing poems in Chinese
1578	Sixth Royal Secretary but, censured by the Easterners, returns home; writes "Little Odes on Mount Star" (c. 1578 or later)
1580	Governor of Kangwŏn province; writes "The Wanderings"
1581	Returns to Seoul to become Rector, National Academy; denounced by opposition for his uncompromising stance, returns to Ch'angp'yŏng (eighth month)
1582	First Royal Secretary; Second Minister of Rites
1583	Minister of Rites
1584	Inspector-General
1585	Leaves his post due to the opposition's criticism of his fondness for wine
1585–1589	Leads life of a recluse; writes "Hymn of Constancy" and "Continued Hymn of Constancy"
1589	Third State Counselor (15 December)
1590	Second State Counselor (9 March)
1591	Provokes the king's ire by proposing Prince Kwanghae as heir apparent; sent into exile

1592	Released from exile (fifth month); hastens to P'yŏngyang and escorts the king to Ŭiju to flee the advancing Japanese army
1593	Envoy to Ming China
1594	Dies on Kanghwa Island at the age of fifty-six (7 February)

KASA

The Wanderings (1580)
[*Kwandong pyŏlgok*]

I lay sick among rivers and lakes,
resting in bamboo groves.
Then the king made me governor
of Kwandong, eight hundred *ri* away.
O royal favor,
unfathomable grace.
I rush through the Prolonging Autumn Gate,[1]
bow toward the South Gate,[2]
bid my lord farewell and withdraw,
and find a man holding a jade tally.[3]
I change horses at Flat Hill Station[4]
and follow the Black River.[5]
Where is the Striped Toad River?[6]
Here Pheasant Mountain[7] rises.
O waters of the Luminous Ether,[8]
whither do you flow?
When a lonely subject leaves the court,
there is nothing left to him but growing old.
    After a sleepless night at Ch'ŏrwŏn,
I climb to Broad North Arbor,[9]
scanning the first peak
of Three Peaked Mountain.
Magpies chattering
at the palace site of Kung Ye,[10]
do you know
the rise and fall of changing ages?
May we witness again
the noble mien of Chi Ch'ang-ju![11]
O my Hoeyang, my town,

Huai-yang of the Former Han.
My hostel is quiet,
it is the third month.
A path along the Flower River
stretches to the Diamond Mountains.
I fling off coat and sack
and let my staff lead me on a stone path
along Hundred Rivers Canyon[12]
to Myriad Falls Grotto.[13]
There silver rainbows,
dragons with jade tails,
turning and coiling, spurt cataracts,
rending the hills ten miles away.
Listen to the thunder;
look, there is snow.

    At the top of Diamond Terrace,[14]
home of immortal cranes,
awakened by spring breeze
and jade flute,
noble birds in white and black silk[15]
soar into midair
to frolic with Lin Pu,
master of the West Lake.[16]
Looking downward at
the peaks like incense burners,
I am at the True Light Temple
on True Rest Terrace.[17]
I can see it all,
the true shape of Mount Lu![18]
Ah, extravagant celestial creator!
What abundance of strange forms!
Some fly, some dash—
some stand, some soar—
as if planting lotus,
bundling white jade,
sifting the Eastern Sea from its bed,

and heaving up the North Pole!
Lofty Height Viewing Terrace[19]
and lonely Cave Viewing Peak[20]
shoot into the blue
and speak to the Maker
from aeons
constant and unbending.
Ah, it could only be you,
we can't match your steadfastness.
   From Open Mind Terrace[21]
I view All Fragrance Castle[22]
and count twelve thousand peaks
in the clear air.
If we could gather the air's vitality,
pure yet clean,
clean yet pure,
on every peak
and every crest
and bring it back to create a man!
O multitudinous, baffling shapes,
come into being of themselves
when heaven and earth first opened.
Now that I look at them
they seem to have feelings.
   Who has ever stood
on the crest of Vairocana Peak?[23]
Which is higher,
Mount Tung or Mount T'ai?[24]
Who said the kingdom of Lu
was small?
Who said all under heaven
appeared to him small?[25]
Ah, how could we know
its limits?
Better descend,
if you cannot gain the summit.

Through a narrow path along the Grotto of Perfect Penetration[26]
I find Lion Peak.[27]
Giant boulders in front form
the Fiery Dragon Pool.
A thousand-year-old dragon,
coiling round and round,
floats day and night
and reaches the open sea.
When will you gain winds and clouds,
and send sweet rain for three days
to yellowing leaves
on a shadowy cliff?
Seeing Maha Chasm, Maitreya on a cliff,[28]
and Goose Gate Hill,[29]
I cross a rotting log bridge
to Buddha's Head Terrace,[30]
a cliff hanging in air
over a thousand fathoms deep.
The Milky Way
unrolls its filaments
showing the warp and woof
of its hemp cloth.
Twelve cascades on nature's map;
but I can see a few more!
Had Li Po been here
and compared two views,
he would not have bragged
of the waterfall at Mount Lu.
    Why linger in the mountains?
Let's go to the Eastern Sea.
A bamboo sedan-chair climbs slowly
to Mountain Glare Tower.[31]
Crying birds
and crystal torrent
hate to part.
Unfurl banners and flags,

five colors brave the sky;
beat the drum and play the flute,
music rolls away clouds and seas.
A horse familiar with singing sand beach
carries the drunken poet aslant
with the sea by his side
to look for clusters of wild roses.
Gulls, don't fly away!
How do you know if I'm your friend or not?
   Circling around Gold Orchid Cave[32]
I climb to Clustered Rock Arbor[33]
and see four pillars
of the palace of White Jade Tower.
Work of a master artisan,[34]
the touch of a magic axe.
What is meant
by its six-sided shape?
Leaving Kosŏng behind,
I reach Three Days Cove.[35]
The six red letters are still on the cliff,
but where are the four knights of Silla?
After three days here
where did they go?
Were they staying at Sŏnyu pool[36]
or by Yŏngnang Lake?[37]
Were they sitting at Clear Torrent Arbor
or on Myriad View Terrace?[38]
   Pear blossoms fall,
a cuckoo calls sadly.
Along the east bank of Mount Nak
I climb to Ŭisang Terrace[39]
and get up at dawn
to await the rising sun.
On the horizon lucky clouds appear;
six dragons uphold and push the sun.
When the sun left the sea,

the whole world shimmered in its light;
now that it shines in midair,
I can count the tiniest hair.
May the clouds
never cover the sunlight.
Yes, Li Po is dead,
but his poems endure.
How subtly he sang of this magnificence
between heaven and earth.
   Continually treading the azaleas
on Steep Hill Mountain[40] in the setting sun,
the noble carriage with feathered top
rolls down to Mirror Cove.[41]
Behind old pines rimming like hedges
I scan a ten-mile-long beach
like ironed and stretched white silk;
the water is calm and clear,
I can count the grains of sand.
I row a solitary boat
and climb to an arbor.
Beyond River Gate Bridge[42]
the ocean is forever placid,
leisurely in temper,
vast in boundary,
unmatched anywhere in the world
in its natural splendor.
People still tell
the tale of Hongjang.[43]
Kangnŭng province,
famed for virtue and good customs—
flagpoles for filial sons
adorn the valleys.
Truly the people of Yao and Shun
still seem to linger here.
   The Fifty River flows to the sea,
below Pearl Harbor and West Bamboo Tower,[44]

mirroring the green
of the Great White Mountains.[45]
Would that I could make it flow
to the Han below Mount South.
Officials' journeys have limits;
only landscapes are infinite.
My heart is full;
I'll brave the wanderer's sorrow—
Should I board the celestial raft
to the Dipper and Herdboy?
Should I go to Cinnabar Cave
to find the four immortals?
To fathom the roots of the *Ti* Star[46]
the poet asks, standing at Sea Viewing Arbor:[47]
"Heaven lies beyond the seas;
what lies beyond heaven?"
Who enraged
the already angered whale?
It blows and spews,
how giddying its tumult!
The silver mountain is leveled;
it crashes in every direction.
What a sight—snow falls
in the boundless sky of the fifth month!
    Unawares night falls,
winds and waves lull.
As I wait for the moon from the east
the horizon seems to draw near.
Lustrous moonlight a thousand feet long,
now there, now gone.
I roll up again a pearl-sewn screen
and sweep the jade stairs;
while I sit erect,
awaiting the morning star,
someone sends me
a spray of white lotus.

O let this world
be revealed to all!
Holding a cup of enchanting wine[48]
I ask the moon:
"Where are the heroes,
who are the four immortal knights?"
No one listens;
I am not answered.
I have miles to travel
on this magic mountain of the Eastern Sea.
    I doze and fall asleep,
my head on the pine trunk.
A voice whispers to me
in my dream:
How could I not know you?
You are a true fairy,
who misread the word
in the Book of the Yellow Court[49]
and was banished from heaven
to the world of men.
But linger on, friend,
taste my immortal wine.
The Dipper for a ladle,
the Ocean for wine,
he himself drinks and offers me a cup.
One cup, two cups, we drink by turns
until the gentle warm breeze
lifts me by the arm
and I can stride into the great void.
Let us divide this wine
among the four seas.
Let the whole world drink
and be in wine.
Then let us meet again
and exchange cups.
Words spoken,

he soared skyward on a crane's back.
Only a jade flute rings in the void.
Was it yesterday or the day before?
Awakening,
I look downward.
I know not the sea's depth
nor its breadth.
Only the bright moon is shining
on a thousand hills and myriad villages.

Hymn of Constancy (c. 1585–1589)
[*Sa miin kok*]

When heaven created this body,
I was born to serve you.
It is a lifetime affinity;
heaven, too, knows it.
I stayed young
and you loved me alone.
Nothing can match
my constancy and your love.
My lifelong wish
was to be with you always.
Why in our old age
do we yearn for each other?
Yesterday I repaired with you
to the Moon Palace,[50]
but for some reason
I fell to the lower world.
My hair, well combed then,
has been disheveled for three years.
I've rouge and powder,
but for whom should I make up?

My mind, knotted in grief,
piled fold upon fold,
only produces sighs,
only brings tears.
Life has an end;
only sorrow is endless.
    Fickle time flows,
flows by like water;
cold and heat
come and go,
as if they know time.
Much to hear and see,
everything stirs deep feeling.
In an instant spring winds
hollow out piled snow,
and two or three plum sprays
blossom outside my window.
They are not only calm and easy,
but send hidden fragrance.
At dusk the moon rises
and shines on my pillow.
Is it feeling and welcoming?
Is it my lord, is it not?
Were I to send him
a plum branch,
what would he think
when he saw it?
    Flowers are gone, leaves open,
and a green shadow adorns the ground.
Gauze curtains are forlorn,
embroidered canopies raised in vain.
Pulling a lotus curtain aside,
I set a peacock screen.
My grief is enough—
O long cruel day!
Cut the silk with mandarin-duck designs,

loosen the thread of five colors,
size it with a golden measure:
I make his clothes
with skill and style,
every detail proper.
On a coral carrier
in a jade box
I'd offer him this garment,
gazing toward his far abode—
mountains are rugged,
clouds are ominous,
who will risk
these thousand miles?
Would he open the box
and welcome it as if it were me?
    When frost falls overnight
and wild geese pass, crying,
I stand on a high tower
rolling up the crystal screen:
the moon rises over the eastern hill,
the polestar glitters in the north—
is it he? I rush out to meet him:
only tears blind my eyes.
Let me seize a handful of clear light
and send it to your phoenix tower.
Hang it atop the tower, please,
let it shine over eight corners,
and make every steep hill and valley
bright as day.
    Now the whole world is frozen;
white snow is everywhere,
both men and birds
have vanished from sight.
When the south banks of the Hsiao and Hsiang[51]
are cold as they are now,
how cold must he be

in that high tower?
Would I might catch spring,
make it shine on him!
Would I might offer him the sunlight
that once shone on my cottage eaves.
Tucking in my red skirt,
rolling up my green sleeves,
I lean on tall bamboo at sunset.
A thousand thoughts are too many.
The day was short;
but at night I sit up
with a mica-inlaid harp
by the hanging blue lamp,
chin in my hand, leaning on a wall,
hoping to dream of him.
O cold is the mandarin-duck embroidered quilt,
long is the night.
    Twelve times a day,
thirty days in the month,
in vain I try, not to think,
but to bury this grief,
tangled in knots
and piercing me to the marrow.
Not even ten Renowned Doctors[52]
can cure my sickness.
This is all, alas,
all due to my lord.
Better to die
and become a butterfly,
stop at each flower,
rest upon each branch,
with scented wings,
and light upon his cloak.
He may not remember me:
yet I will follow him.

Continued Hymn of Constancy (c. 1585–1589)
[*Sok miin kok*]

"Lady, who goes there?
You look so familiar.
Why did you leave
the White Jade Capital in the heavens,[53]
whom do you seek
as the sun goes down?"

"Oh, it's you!
Hear my story now.
My face and ways
do not merit my lord's favor.
Yet he deigns to recognize me
when we meet.
I believed in him
with undivided heart.
I flirted and displayed my charm—
I might have annoyed him.
His welcoming face
has changed from the past.
Reclining, I ponder;
seated, I calculate:
my sins,
piled high as the mountains;
I don't quarrel with heaven,
I don't blame men.
I try to untie this sadness—
it was the Fashioner's doing."

"Fret not, my dear.
Something eats at my heart, too.
I've served him;
I know him.
His face once placid as water

shows little enough of peace these days.
Spring cold and summer heat,
how did he spend them?
Autumn days and winter skies,
who served them?
Morning gruel and daily rice,
did he have enough?
Do you think he slept well
these long winter nights?"

"I yearn for word of him,
how I long to hear his news!
But the day is done.
Will someone come tomorrow?
O tormenting thought!
Where shall I go?
Led and pushed
when I climb a high hill,
clouds gather,
and—why—a mist, too!
When hills and waters are dark,
how can I see the sun and moon?
What can I see even an inch away?
A thousand miles is so far . . .
I'll go down to the sea
and wait for a boat.
Winds and waves
in turmoil, in shambles.
The boatman is gone;
only the empty ship . . .
Standing alone by the river,
I gaze far into the setting sun.
News from my lord
is out of the question!
I return when darkness creeps
under the eaves of my hut.

For whom does that lamp
in the middle of the wall burn?
Over hill and valley I go,
back and forth, aimlessly.
Exhausted,
I sink into sleep.
At last my prayer is answered,
and I see him in a dream.
But time has stolen
his face once like jade.
I would tell him all,
all my heart desires.
But tears flow on and on,
and I cannot speak.
Unable to tell of my love,
words stick in my throat.
A frivolous rooster
wakes me from my slumber.
Ah, everything was a mocking dream.
Where is my fair one?
Sitting up in my sleep,
I open the window.
Only the pitiable shadow
follows me.
I'd sooner die
and be the setting moon
and shine
in his window."

"The moon say you, my lady?
Rather, a driving rain."[54]

Little Odes on Mount Star (c. 1578)
[*Sŏngsan pyŏlgok*]

An unknown guest in passing
stopped on Mount Star and said:
"Listen, Master of Mist Settling Hall
and Resting Shadow Arbor,
despite the many pleasures
life held,
why did you prefer to them all
this mountain, this water?
What made you choose
the solitude of hills and streams?"
    Sweeping away the pine needles,
setting a cushion on a bamboo couch,
I casually climb into the seat
and view the four quarters.
Floating clouds at the sky's edge come and go
nestling on Auspicious Stone Terrace;⁵⁵
their flying motion and gentle gestures
resemble our host.
White waves in the blue stream
rim the arbor,
as if someone stitched and spread
the cloud brocade of the Weaver Star,
the water rushes
in endless patterns.
In other mountains without a calendar
who would know the year's cycle?
Here every subtle change of the seasons
unrolls before us.
Whether you hear or see,
this is truly the land of immortals.
    The morning sun at the window with plum trees—
the fragrance of blossoms wakes me.

Who says there is nothing
to keep an old hermit busy?
In the sunny spot under the hedges
I sow melons,
tie the vines, support them;
when rain nurtures the plants,
I think of the old tale
of the Blue Gate.[56]
Tying my straw sandals,
grasping a bamboo staff,
I follow the peach blossom causeway
over to Fragrant Grass Islet.
As I stroll to the West Brook,
the stone screen painted by nature
in the bright moonlit mirror
accompanies me.
Why seek Peach Blossoms Spring?[57]
Earthly paradise is here.
    The casual south wind
scatters green shade;
a faithful cuckoo,
where did he come from?
I wake from dozing
on the pillow of ancient worthies[58]
and see the hanging wet balcony
floating on the water.
With my kudzu cap aslant
and my hemp smock tucked into my belt,
I go nearer
to watch the frolicking fishes.
After the rain overnight,
here and there, red and white lotus;
their fragrance rises into the still sky
filling myriad hills.
As though I had met with Chou Tun-i[59]
and questioned him on the Ultimate Secret—

as though an immortal Great Unique[60]
had shown me the Jade Letters—
I look across Cormorant Rock
by Purple Forbidden Shallows;
a tall pine tree screens the sun,
I sit on the stone path.
In the world of man it is the sixth month;
here it is autumn.
A duck bobbing on the limpid stream
moves to a white sandbar,
makes friends with the gulls,
and dozes away.
Free and leisurely,
it resembles our host.
    At the fourth watch the frost moon rises
over the phoenix trees.
Thousand cliffs, ten thousand ravines,
could they be brighter by daylight?
Who moved the Crystal Palace
from Hu-chou?[61]
Did I jump over the Milky Way
and climb into the Moon Palace?
Leaving behind a pair of old pines
on the fishing terrace,
I let my boat drift downstream
as it pleases,
passing pink knotweeds
and a sandbar of white cloverfern.
When did we reach
the Dragon Pool below Jade Ring Hall?
Moved by a sunset glow,
cowherds
in green pastures by the crystal river
blow on their pipes.
They might awaken the dragon
sunk deep at the pool's bottom.

Emerging from mists and ripples,
cranes might abandon their nests
and soar into midair.
Su Shih in his poem on Red Cliff
praises the seventh moon;[62]
but why do people cherish
the mid-autumn moon?
When thin clouds part,
and waves grow still,
the rising moon
anchors herself in a pine branch.
How extravagant! Li Po drowned
trying to scoop up the reflected moon.

   North winds sweep away
the heaped leaves on empty hills,
marshal the clouds,
drive the snow.
The Creator loves to fashion—
he makes snowflowers of white jade,
devises thousands of trees and forests.
The shallows in front freeze over.
A monk crosses over
the one-log bridge aslant,
a staff on his shoulder.
What temple are you headed for?

   Don't boast of
the recluse's riches
lest some find out
this lustrous, hidden world.
Alone, deep in the mountains,
with the classics, pile on pile,
I think of the men
of all times:
many were sages,
many were heroes.
Heavenly intention goes

into the making of men.
Yet fortunes
rise and fall;
chance seems unknowable.
And sadness deep.
Why did Hsü Yu on Mount Chi
cleanse his innocent ears?[63]
When he threw away his last gourd,
his integrity became even nobler.
    Man's mind is like his face—
new each time one sees it.
Worldly affairs are like clouds—
how perilous they are!
The wine made yesterday
must be ready:
passing the cup back and forth,
let's pour more wine till we're tired.
Then our hearts will open,
the net of sorrow unravel to nothing.
String the black zither
and pluck "Wind in the Pines."[64]
We have all forgotten
Who is host and who is guest.
The crane flying through the vast sky
is the true immortal in this valley—
I must have met him
on the Jasper Terrace under the moon.
The guest addresses the host with a word:
"You, sir, you alone are immortal."

A Time to Drink
[*Chang chinju sa*]

Let's drink a cup,
and then another.
Let's pluck flowers and count
as we drink more and more.
When your body dies,
it will be borne on a rack
wrapped around with a straw mat,
or in a hearse with colored curtains,
with myriad people following in tears.
And when you're laid down
among the rushes,
under overcup oaks and white poplars,
under yellow sun and white moon,
under fine rain or thick snow,
or when chilly winds sough,
who will offer you a cup of wine?
Furthermore, when only a monkey whistles
on your grave,
what good will it do to regret?

SIJO

1

My father got me;
My mother bore me:
Without them I would not
Exist at all.
How can I ever show my thanks
For the heavenly gift of life?[1]

2

The sovereign is heaven,
His subjects, the earth.
He wishes to know
All our grievances.
How could we then eat alone
Even the succulent parsley?

3

Brothers,
Feel your bodies.
Who has made you two alike?
Even your appearance is the same.
You grew up in the same bosom;
Never harbor treacherous designs.

4

While your parents still live,
Be as filial as you can.
What use to regret and grieve
After they have passed away?
This alone you cannot repair:
You cannot redeem want of piety.

5

Divide one body in two parts:
Thus the creator made man and wife.
The two grow old together in life;
The two lie together in the grave.
No foolish words and deeds,
Nor exchange scowls in your old age.

6

If you meet young girls on your path,
Be sure to make a detour.
If you meet young men on your way,
Be sure to turn back.
If the person is not your man or girl,
Do not ask his or her name.

7

How far has your son advanced
With the *Book of Filial Piety?*
The day after tomorrow my son will
Finish reading the *Elementary Learning.*
When will they master these books?
When will we see them become gentlemen?

8

O villagers, let us be honest
And upright in our deeds.
Once you depart from the true way,
Though born into this world as men,
How do you differ from horses and oxen
Wearing caps and cowls and eating rice?

9

When an elder grasps your wrist,
Help him to his feet.
When he wishes to go out,
Follow him with his staff.
When the village feast is over,
Be sure to take him home.

10

No one is more trustworthy than a friend
Among those unrelated by blood.
He points out all my errors
And reasons with me.
How can I make myself a man
Without such a true friend?

11

O nephews: what if
You have no rice to cook?
O uncles: what if
You have no clothes to wear?
Tell me all about your needs;
I'll hasten to help you.

12

How much have you prepared
For the family's mourning rites?
When will you choose mates
For your own daughters?
Although we are not well off,
We would like to help you.

13

Another day is dawning;
Let us go to the field with hoes.
After weeding my fields,
I shall help you weed yours.
And on our way home we shall pick
Mulberry leaves for the silkworms.

14

Even if you have no clothes,
Do not take another's by force.
Even if you have no grain,
Do not beg for another's rice.
If you are soiled just once,
It is hard to cleanse yourself again.

15

Do not bet on dice or chess,
Nor litigate with others;
Or you will be brought to ruin
And make new enemies.
The state has enacted laws
To punish men for their crimes.

16

Let me help you, old man,
With packs on your head and back.
Because I am young,
I could even carry stones for you.
Just growing old must be sorrowful;
Why carry your burden around?

17

O people of Kangwŏn province,
Let no brothers sue one another.
Servants and fields are easily bought,
But not blood ties.
Why glare at one another,
When brotherhood is hard to find?

18

Once I entered Kwanghwa Gate
In the night-duty office of the Royal Guards
I would hear twenty-three drumbeats
At the fifth watch.[2]
This is already a thing of the past;
Was it a dream?

19

From the palace precinct[3]
The drums toll the fifth watch.
Their resonance crosses the walls and clouds
And strikes my ear at an inn.
But once I go south of the river,
How will I hear that familiar beat?

20

The juice of bitter herbs has
More taste than any meat.
My small grass hut is
A fitting abode for me.
But my longing for my lord
chokes me with grief.

21

When did Liu Ling live?[4]
He was a lofty man of Chin.
Who is that man named Kyeham?[5]
He is a dissolute fellow of the day.
What good is there to discriminate
A worthy or a profligate?

22

Listen, members of the family:
How are you going to live?
You have eaten the husks of grain
And used up the very last gourds.
Whom can you depend on
When your master lives loose?

23

Whether I have drunk too much
And weave my way down the street,
Or my family is in great disorder
Without a single gourd cup,
I will live on with confidence
If my king deigns to love me.

24

I have been your friend for ten years—
God knows why.
I have followed you with nothing achieved,
And now you question my integrity.
Suppose I send you off
With a dirge on the rupture of our ties?[6]

25

If you wanted a worldly career,
Why did you befriend me?
You welcomed me whenever you saw me;
So I followed you around.
If you say these ties are wrong,
Why not sever them now?

26

Listen once again to my words:
I cannot live without you.
I can forget because of you
The harsh and rugged things in life.
How could I now abandon you
To love someone else?

27

Suppose you lived a hundred years;
Would it not be troublesome?
Then for what end and with what intent
In this hard floating life
Do you refuse the cup I offer
And do not drink it down?

28

Were I to spread my wings here
And flap them twice or thrice,
I could see my beloved lord
On the loftiest peak of Mount Pongnae.
But what good is it to prate
About what you can and cannot do?

29

I would like to break up this body
And let its pieces float down the stream.
If this water were to flow on sobbing
To become rapids of the Han,
Then only could I cure this disease
Of yearning for my lord.

30

I wish I could halve my heart
And make it into a moon.
Then hung perfectly
In ninety-thousand-league heaven,
I would travel to my beloved lord's abode
And shine down upon him.

31

Countless rises and falls of fortune!
Thick grows the autumn grass in Taebang.[7]
Let the shepherd's pipe
Sing of events now long forgotten.
Won't you try a cup
In this peaceful and happy age?

32

When Shin was Fifth Counselor,[8]
I was in the sixth rank.
We took turns at night watch
Outside the palace's South Gate.
Now only the jade face of my beloved lord
Flickers before my eyes.

33

Upon Resting Shadow Arbor,
Old Man of the South Pole shines.[9]
Even when mulberry fields have become a sea
And everything has overturned,
This star shines the brighter;
It never dims its light.

34

How many years has it grown,
That elm tree on the terrace?
Until the tender tree grows older,
From a seed that has sprouted,
I will pour another cup
And pray for your long life.

35

O crane, you have soared high
Beyond the clouds in the blue sky.
For what reason do you alight?
Do you long for the human world?
You know how to fly away
Until your long wings shed their feathers.

36

The third string on the Black Zither
Softens my spirit and soothes.
I then play the rapid finale
On the second string.
Its sound is not at all sad,
So I cannot part from you.

37

You wheel around, crane,
Until you shed your white feathers.
And soaring high among the clouds,
You speak:
"I shall soar and soar again
Until I have glimpsed the cosmos."

38

As a Stage Warden in Sinwŏn[10]
I receive the traveling guests.
Coming and going,
Numerous are their greetings.
How tiresome
To sit and watch them.

39

I am a Stage Warden in Sinwŏn.
Wearing a sedge cape and reed cap
In the fine rain and slanting wind,
With a rod on my shoulder
I wander about the shores
Amid pink knotweed and white cloverfern.

40

I am still a Stage Warden,
Yet I close my brushwood door behind me
And give myself over to my friends—
Green hills and flowing waters.
If an official comes from Pyŏkche,
Tell him I have gone out.

41

How absurd is the story
Of Chia Yi the Grand Tutor.[11]
He alone bore
Others' grief.
Sighs and tears are more than enough;
Why must you lament aloud?

42

When you climb bends of Mount Sumeru,[12]
They say, at high noon in midsummer,
There is a severe frost and heavy snow falls
On a ground rimmed with ice.
Have you seen this, my lord,
With your own eyes?
No matter what everyone else says,
Please use your own judgment.

43

I know easily that
My looks fall behind others'.
Therefore I give up rouge,
White powder and black pencil.
This plain self
Will not dream of winning his love.

44

Now that the big tree is sick,
The arbor is bare of guests.
Travelers loved to rest
Under the tree lustrous and green.
Now, not even the birds alight
On the leafless and broken tree.

45

O, hewn,
Hewn is the tall and hardy pine.
It would have yielded beams
Had we left the tree longer.
When the Royal Hall declines,
What tree will support the state?

46

Yesterday they told me the wine was ripe
In Mr. Sŏng's house over the hill.[13]
So I kick a sleeping ox awake,
Put on a saddlecloth and mount up.
"Boy, is your master at home?
Tell him Overseer Chŏng is here."

47

After ten years I admire again
The jade cup in Hongmun Hall.[14]
Its limpid white color
Has not changed as time passed.
But why does the mind of man
Play us false morning and night?

48

How could you leave it to rot,
Lumber fit for beams and rafters?
Small men indulge in hot debate
In a tumbledown shack.
O carpenters with ink cup and measure,
You rush about to no avail.

49

If you suppress a coy smile,
A sneeze will tickle your nose.
If you play the coquette halfheartedly,
You may lose out in love.
Before the sweet wine is ripe,
Let us not think of other matters.

50

Do not heave sighs and say,
"I shall depart" or "I shall stay."
Do not laugh a forced laugh and say,
"You are drunk" or "You are sober."
Would you be quieter on a rainy day,
If I removed your cape and detained you?

51

Let us strain sour wine and drink
Until our mouths become sour.
Let us steam bitter herbs and chew them
Until they turn sweet.
Let us walk around
Until the nails in our clogs have worn flat.

52

The soaring pagoda—lofty throughout
Silla's eight hundred years.
The boom of the thousand-pound bell;
How clear is each tolling!
The sound crosses the field
To enliven the dusk in a desolate arbor.

53

A dash of rain upon
The lotus leaves. But the leaves
Remain unmarked, no matter
How hard the raindrops beat.
Mind, be like the lotus leaves,
Unstained by the world.

54

A crane has flown away;
The arbor is empty.
When shall I return
If I take this road now?
I will empty a cup
Between my coming and going.

55

Wash and wash again
My only raw silk jacket.
Dry it in baking sun;
Iron it with care.
Drape it over your shoulders,
Smooth and tenderly fashioned!

56

Mr. Ko builds a grass hut[15]
Somewhere on South Mountain.
He tends flowers and the moon,
And stones and water.
He must keep wine also;
He invites me in for a cup.

57

My old love is new love,
Her airs and graces remain the same.
—Was all a dream,
A trace of long ago?
If my heart had changed,
I could have looked away when you came.

58

I am fifty, but I am not old.
I see wine wherever I go
And grin at its presence.
Do not press me why.
I cannot forget you; we have
Known each other just too long.

59

Is it from the beginning that
I have been so frivolous?
The thing begun in fun
Has become a serious matter.
I sit up from my sleep,
Often startled by this.

60

Would I envy others' laughter,
Neglecting my troubles?
Would I join in another's party,
Leaving a cup of my wine?
Would I change my first love,
My heart fresh as jade?

61

Do not wake a sleeping baby—
You cannot hush a crying child.
He pulls for his mother's breast
And keeps on crying.
It is not becoming to an adult to say,
"There, there. Don't cry."

62

Let forty thousand pecks of pearls
Rest on the lotus leaves.
I box them and measure them
To send them off somewhere.
Tumultuous rolling drops—
How zestful, graceful.

63

I have idled my time away
And roamed here and there.
My words and deeds lack conviction;
I have achieved nothing.
What is done is done.
Why not enjoy the rest of my life?

64

On a windy, frosty day
He grants to Hongmun Hall
Yellow chrysanthemums
On a silver platter.
O fickle peach and plum blossoms,
Can you fathom his intent?[16]

65

I press the second note on the third string
Of the Black Zither.
The sound surges like a stream freed of ice
Rushing up from the shallows.
Distant raindrops, too, play in concert;
They beat on lotus leaves.

66

I know autumn has come:
The phoenix tree has shed its leaves.
Cool is the night,
A silken rain falls on the clear river.
My love is a thousand miles away;
I cannot sleep.

67

I bade you farewell when
Fallen leaves danced in the autumn wind.
Now snow and ice have melted,
And spring flowers have blossomed.
But you send me no word—
How sad, my love!

68

Last night over Wu-ling Hills
Under threatening clouds
A pair of phoenix dallied
In amorous pursuit.
They dropped a feather here and there,
But don't look to find them on this earth.

69

O flap-eared horse
Starting out for the salt pond:
You were once a swift steed
That made a thousand miles a day.
But people today only know
That you have become fat!

70

O kite, take away
All misfortune from our family.
And, aloof from the human world
On a lone tree in the field,
Wear yourself out on a day
Of rain and wind.[17]

71

Snow falls on a pine grove;
Every branch blossoms.
I wish I could break off a branch
To send to my lord.
No matter if the blossoms fade
After he has seen my branch.

72

A shadow on the stream—
A monk crosses the bridge.
Stop awhile, cowled traveler.
Where will your journey take you?
He does not turn around, but walks on
Pointing to white clouds with his stick.

73

Boys have gone out to gather bracken;
The bamboo grove is empty.
Who will pick up the dice
Scattered on the checkerboard?
Drunk, I lean on a pine trunk
And let dawn pass me by.

74

If I were a remarkable man,
He would not have given me up.
Had I been a common officer,
I could have followed him.
I am not even a common officer;
When can I see him then?

75

Flowers are bright, bright;
Butterflies fly in pairs.
Willows are green, green;
Orioles sing in pairs.
Birds and beasts love in twos;
Why do I live alone?

76

Milky rain on the green hills,
Can you deceive me?
Sedge cape and horsehair hat,
Can you deceive me?
Yesterday I flung off my silk robe.
I have nothing left that will stain me.

77

Birds fly home to roost;
The new moon rises.
A lonely cowled traveler
Passes over a log bridge.
How far is your temple?
Do you hear distant drums?

78

In the slanting evening sun,
Sky and river are a single color.
O cackling geese flying among
The burning maples and feathery reeds.
Autumn is almost gone;
He still keeps silent.

79

Two stone Buddhas on the wayside
Without clothes and food—
You weather wind and rain,
You brave snow and frost.
You do not know the wrench of parting.
In this I envy you most.

*

I bemoan the death of my husband,
And tears course down my bosom.
I cannot still my crying child;
He complains that the milk is too salty.
"O wretched baby,
What is woman supposed to do?"[18]

Where did the ship vanish,
Tossed about by wind and waves?
They should not have set out
Under threatening clouds.
Owners of worn-out ships,
You must all take caution.

O pine tree standing there,
Why do you live by the roadside?
Move yourself a little and
Stay in that hollow a while.
Watch the men with rope and axe—
They want to cut you down.

Pak Illo

1561 Born in Toch'ŏn, Yŏngyang, as the eldest son of Pak Sŏk (1 August)

1592 Joins the army under Sŏng Yunmun (fl. 1591–1607)

1598 Writes "Song of Peace"

1599 Passes military service examination; appointed *manho* (myriarch) at Chorap'o

1601 Writes "Early Red Persimmons"

1605 Navy captain in Pusan; writes "Lament on the Water"; military career ends

1611 Visits Yi Tŏkhyŏng (1561–1613) and writes "Song of the Sedge Bank" and "In Praise of Poverty"

1619 Writes "The Hall of Solitary Bliss" to praise Yi Ŏnjŏk (1491–1553); two poems on "Pepper Well," which he visited with Chŏng Ku (1543–1620)

1629 Writes "Twenty-nine Songs on the Standing Rock," where Chang Hyŏngwang (1554–1637) had a retreat

1635 Writes "Song of the Southeast" to praise Yi Kŭnwŏn's good administration

1636 Writes "Song of the Reedy Stream"; "Songs of the Five Relations" (after 1634); and "Thinking of Parents and Other Poems" (c. 1636)

1643 Dies on 25 January

KASA

Song of Peace (1598)
[*T'aep'yŏng sa*]

Long and narrow, our land remained secluded
to the east of the Yellow Sea.
Through the ages we followed
the pure and honest ways of Chi Tzu.[1]
For two centuries since the dynasty's founding,
we upheld the rites and justice,
and our civilization matched
the glory of Han, T'ang, and Sung.
But one morning
a million island savages
clashed with millions of innocent souls,
resolved to follow the glint of the sword.
Bones lay in heaps
on the plain,
majestic cities and imposing towns
became lairs for wolves and foxes.
Cold and lonely,
the royal carriage sped north
in the smoke and dust
that gauzed the sunlight.
    The Ming emperor, marvelous and valiant,
cast a deadly roar
and cut down with a single sword
the wicked Japanese raiders at P'yŏngyang.
Like the wind he spurred his troops southward,
pressing the enemy hard to the shore.
We did not storm the cornered pirates,[2]
but besieged them for several years.

And to the east of the Naktong River
the pick of our army, like lofty clouds,
met a great tactician and general,[3]
and under his five brilliant virtues[4]
our soldiers became hunters of wild dogs.
The humanity and bravery of our heroes
blended with the eloquence of a mediator.[5]
Peace settled again in the south,
and soldiers and horses gathered strength, waiting.
     But one evening
a storm broke again,
and generals like dragons,
soldiers like clouds,
under the royal standard that covered the sky[6]
spread out along frontiers myriad miles long.
Hills shook
with the battle cry;
generals led the van
and rushed the enemy
like thunderbolts in a tempest.
Callow Captain Kiyomasa[7]
was in our grasp;
but tired soldiers,
in the trying rain,
raised the siege,
stiffened morale.
The raiders then ran in the four directions;
we may not catch them all alive.
Their caves,
once so strong,
are now heaps of ashes—
a natural fastness is not all in a battle.[8]
Since the lofty virtue of the Son of Heaven
and the abundant favors of our king
extend far and near,
heaven punished the wily bandits with death

and manifested humanity and justice.
Was it yesterday that we sang of peace?[9]
Even the idle
became his majesty's men,
fought desperately to repay his favor,
fought east and west for seven years
to lay down their lives for their country.
Today, once again, peace reigns over the land,
and we return to the willowed barracks[10]
putting our spears aside.
Songs of peace
and drums and horns
are loud as the laughter of dragons and fishes
that reside deep in the Palace of the Dragon King.
Royal banners, too, in the west wind
flutter aslant,
like five-hued lucky clouds
hanging in the sky.
A scene of peace
spreads endless and happy.
Raising the bow, lifting the arrow,
we sing the triumphal chant
as if to outdo one another.
Our joyous song gathers in the emerald sky.
Overcome with joy,
with three-foot sword, keen and bright,
I lift my face and whistle a tune;
when I stand up ready to dance,
the magic sword that I lifted high
shines between the Plow and the Weaver.
Hands dance, feet leap,
naturally,
as we praise and dance the seven martial virtues[11]
never wishing to stop.
Of all the joyous things in life,
is there anything like this?

Where is Mount Hua?[12]
I'll dispatch the news.
Where is Mount T'ai?[13]
I'll suspend an arrow on it.
  Now let's be
loyal and filial.
Idle,
I lie asleep in the camp
and ask
in what dynasty I live.
The golden days of Fu Hsi,[14] of course.
As heaven does not send down a long rain,
the sun grows brighter.
The bright white sun
shines upon the world.
Old men scattered
in ditches and moats[15]
return home[16]
like swallows on the spring breeze.
Who would not feel happy
when they can't forget their hometown!
Tell me of the joy
of your return;
O unscathed people,[17]
think of the royal favor that saved you.
Under his profound grace,
brighten the five norms,
nurture the people to build up the nation's power—
they would then rise and march on their own.
  Heaven, we know,
returned luck to favor us.
So we pray that you bless our dynasty;
that the royal house be endless;
that the sun and moon of the Three Dynasties[18]
shine on the golden age of Yao and Shun;
that there be no more war

for myriad years;
that people till the field and dig wells
and sing the praises of peace;[19]
that we always have a holy king above us;
and that he and we share the joy of peace.

Lament on the Water (1605)
[*Sŏnsang t'an*]

My king summoned this sick and aged body
and dispatched me as a shipmaster.
Thus do I travel down to Pusan
in the sultry summer month of the *ŭlsa* year.[20]
Sick as I am, I dare not sit still
in this gateway, the strategic portal.
Wearing a long sword aslant
boldly I step aboard the warship,
muster my courage
and stare with scorn at Tsushima.
The yellow clouds that chase the winds
are gathered up here, gathered up there,
and the dim green waves
and the endless sky are one.
    I wander about on the ship
recalling the past;
my foolish mind
reproaches the Yellow Emperor.[21]
Since the boundless sea
surrounds heaven and earth,
what barbarians will cross
myriad miles of winds and waves
and dare to encroach upon our shores?
Why on earth did people

learn to build ships?
Throughout the ages,
everywhere under heaven,[22]
they have become an endless evil,
fostering sorrow in the people's heart.
Ah, I realize now
it is the First Emperor's fault.
Granted that ships had to be made,
if the Japanese were not bred there,
would empty ships have started out
for Tsushima by themselves?
The First Emperor believed in empty words
and sent maidens and boys to solitary isles[23]
to procure the pills of immortality.
Thus he spawned unruly bandits
on those islands[24]
and brought great indignation and shame
upon the Middle Kingdom.
How many immortality pills
did he obtain,
and did they bring him a life
long as the Great Wall he built?
He, too, was a mortal,
I cannot see what he gained.
     When I consider the matter carefully,
Hsü Shih[25] and his like went too far.
Could he seek refuge elsewhere
as a loyal subject?
He did not see the spirits;
but had he returned,
our naval men
would not have lamented at all.
     Forget them all!
No use to blame the past.
Let's stop this idle dispute
between right and wrong.

Calmly I meditate:
I was too obstinate.
The shipbuilding of the Yellow Emperor
was not so bad after all.
Had there been no ships,
how could Chang Han[26] rouse his spirits
when the autumn breeze caresses him,
how could he return south of the river,
when the sky is clear and the sea broad?
How can a fisherman travel
without a boat
to enjoy his life free as duckweed,
a life better than that of three dukes,[27]
among matchless hills and waters?
    Judging from these,
a system of ships
seems worthy of praise.
And why should we not be elated
sitting astride a darting boat
day and night
as we sing of the moon fronting the winds?
In olden days
wine tables crowded ships;[28]
today,
only large swords and long spears.
A ship it is,
but not as ships once were.
Therefore sorrow and joy,
too, differ.
    From time to time
I gaze at the polestar;[29]
the tears of an old man
deplore the age.
Our civilization
is bright as Han, T'ang, and Sung.
But fortune deserted our dynasty,

and the crafty designs of pirates
made us harbor lasting regrets.
We've not yet wiped out this shame,
not even one hundredth.
However incapable,
I am your subject.
The way of success being different today,
I have grown old without serving at your side.
    But my anxious heart
is always with you.
Firmness of will and apprehension for my country
grow stronger as I grow old.
Insignificant and ill
as I am,
when can I cleanse this shame
and redress this grief?
The dead Chu-ko Liang
chased the living Ssu-ma I,[30]
and the limbless Sun Pin
captured P'ang Chüan.[31]
How then should I—
still alive, four limbs intact—
should I fear
thieves of mice and dogs?
When I charge the enemy ships,
descend upon them,
they'll be fallen leaves
in frosty winds.
By freeing them and seizing them seven times[32]
we too will succeed like Chu-ko Liang.
    O wriggling island savages,
beg quickly for surrender!
You know those who yield are set free—
so yield now and avoid disaster.
The eminent virtues of our king
dictate that all men live together.

In a peaceful world,
we live under another sage ruler,
with his virtues
bright as the sun and moon.
And we who have ridden on battle ships
will soon sing in a fishing boat
in autumn moon and spring breeze,
and laying our heads on high pillows,
we'll see once more the happy era
when all the waters sing in unison.[33]

Song of the Sedge Bank (1611)
[*Saje kok*]

You raised this stupid, clumsy self,
my lord; your good graces were great.
Bowed down, I exhausted my energy[34]
resolved to die for our country.
Day and night, ever mindful, unflagging,[35]
I pondered the course of our dynasty;
but a torch cannot brighten
the sun and moon.
How many years have I neglected my duties
while drawing my salary?
	Sick and old as I was,
you let me leave you;
so to the east of the Han River
I seek the hills and waters
to the Sedge Bank
by the Dragon Ford River.
Abandoned,
unsurpassed nature is without a host;
but familiar are

the color of waters and the hue of hills
where my cherished dream would take me.
Therefore these mindless hills and waters
seem to breathe out warmth.
    O gulls,
playing in threes and fives
on white sand by the bank
veiled in a dim spring dusk,
don't be startled.
Let me ask you
if you too chose this lovely spot.
The emerald waves are wide and deep—
are they not the I and the Wei?[36]
The storied peaks are high—
are they not Mounts Fu-ch'un and Chi?[37]
Forests are deep and roads dark—
are they not Cloud Valley of Chu Hsi?[38]
Springs are sweet and the soil rich—
are they not P'an Valley of Li Yüan?[39]
I wander about and ponder,
but I know not where I stand.
    Irises by the cliff, orchids on the bank,[40]
their hidden fragrance floats far and near,
and the petals fall thick and wide
on the south ravine and east stream.
Clearing out brambles and thorns,
I build a grass hut
and invite my mother, thus fulfilling
a son's duty till the last.
So I learn today I am the only host
among these hills and streams
that I wouldn't exchange
for the titles of three dukes.
Gulls and herons wheeling everywhere,
numberless stags and hinds,
these are the cattle[41]

that *I* raise here;
and the unsold breeze and unsold moon,
they too naturally belong to me.
My riches are
not as other riches.
With my priceless nature,
should I envy the world's riches?
Since I don't know how to envy,
should I be fond of company?
Now that the red dust recedes,
I won't hear or see worldly affairs.
    But without budding flowers and falling leaves
who would know the changes of seasons?
When the bell from Chungŭn Cloister,
riding the valley winds,
through the plum blossoms at my window knocks,
I awaken from a nap, and with sick eyes
see the blossoms opened by rain at night.
Their hidden fragrance
tells of the vernal awakening.
Towards the end of spring,
with new spring robes
and a goosefoot staff,
with six or seven uncapped boys,[42]
I walk, slow and heavy,
across the young grass.
I wash my feet in the crystal stream.
By the bank where the winds are fresh,
elated, I return home singing.
I don't envy Tseng Hsi's joys.
    The pleasure of spring is so,
but no less great is the joy of autumn.
When the golden wind, chill and lonely,
pierces the edge of the garden,
the fall of the phoenix tree leaves
startles even deaf ears.

Just in time meeting the autumn winds,
with delight in my heart,
a rod slung over my shoulder,
I open the pink knotweed bush
and untie a boat
letting it float down to the shallows,
guided by wind and waves.
When the sun sets,
a riverful of rising winds
seems to speed my boat home,
leaving the front hills far behind.
In an instant I become an immortal
sailing on a boat of lotus leaves.
Can Su Shih's trip to the Red Cliff
compare with my blessed pleasure?[43]
Nor can Chang Han's return south of the river
match the splendor of today.
　　Since life by the water is so,
I can easily imagine the delight of the hills.
When late autumn assails the mountain study,
unable to master my inmost thoughts,
with a cane I climb
up a stony path on Mount Ungil,
ramble about as I please,
with monkeys and cranes as my companions.
Then I lean on the tall pine trunk
and scan the four corners.
How artfully the Creator fashions[44]
the mountain scenery!
White clouds and clear mist
drift piece by piece,
settling on every peak and valley,
and frost-laden maple leaves
are redder than spring blossoms.
Screens of brocade
stretched fold upon fold,

a thousand and ten thousand forms
seem to roll in luxury.
If I were to fight for these,
I might not win them;
but since no one prevents my pleasure here,
I can leisurely enjoy the shifting views.
　　At the foot of South Mountain
I plant five grains.
Not enough, you say;
but I never starve.
How delicious is
my corn in my hut!
Add sweet herbs and various fishes
and you would find nothing lacking in the valley.
Not enough delicacies, I know;
but I'll serve my mother here
and show her the virtue of a young crow.[45]
　　Retired as I am from the court
for reasons of my own,
how can I forget for a moment
the vast favor of our beloved king?
The subject's true heart deepens
even as my hair turns gray.
When I raise my head
toward the polestar,
secret tears
often wet my sleeves.
　　Seeing these tears, you would say
I should not have left him behind.
But in this body of limited talent
only sickness seems to thrive.
My mother in the northern chamber
too nears her eightieth year.
So here I must brew magic herbs,
waiting on her day and night.[46]
My life being so,

when can I leave the hill?
No, I'll serve her and age with her
with the cleansed ears of Hsü Yu,
with the costumes of Lao Lai Tzu,[47]
until the pines have turned to green iron,
the pines thick in the stream out front.

In Praise of Poverty (1611)
[*Nuhang sa*]

Foolish and impractical am I;
no man is more so.
I leave to heaven
weal or woe,
and deep in this mean lane[48]
build myself a grass hut,
cook some rice, or make gruel
in windy morning and rainy evening
with straw wet from wind and rain.
But why so much smoke, volumes of it?
I offer my empty stomach
only lukewarm rice brew.
Although my days are spent so,
should a man go against his will?
Poor but unperturbed,
I try to live as I see fit.
But as time goes on,
little things upset my plan.
    If autumn is short,
let spring be plentiful.
If my pocket is empty,
let my bottle be full.
I'm not the only poor man

between heaven and earth.
Let hunger and cold threaten my body;
sincerity's bright red burns in me still.
For the common good, with no thought of self,
imbued with public spirit,
with knapsacks and bags[49]
full of small provisions,
I took to the field
to die in the last ditch.
For five years I fought my country's battles,
stepped over bodies that lay in heaps,
forded a river of blood.
So went my days;
my house was untended.
    An old, long-bearded retainer[50]
forgets the status of master and servant.
Who will tell me
spring is here?[51]
Whom should I ask
to plow the field?
An old man farms there, sows and reaps;
that's my lot.
See the old farmer outside Yu-hsin,[52]
see the old farmer on a hillock.[53]
No one will say he is lowly,
but however much I may wish to plow,
can I do it without an ox?
    After the long drought,
it's already too late.
But to the field on the high west bank,
I bring water halfway from a puddle,
sourceless water on the road,
left by a passing shower,
and wend a moonless path at dusk,
huffing and puffing,
to one who has half promised

to lend me an ox.
Standing alone
outside the firmly closed gate,
I cough loudly
for a while.
"Who's there?"
"Shameless me."
"What has brought you here
after the first watch?"
"It's improper
to come every year, I know;
but I'm worried
sick about my poor household."
"I would let you use it
for nothing or for a little,
but last night
my neighbor across the way invited me
for a red pheasant cock
broiled on a charcoal fire
dripping with juices,
he plied me with new wine
till I was tipsy.
How could I not repay
such kindness?
I have promised
my ox to him tomorrow.
So I can't break my word.
What else can I tell you?"
If this is so, I say,
What can I do?
With old straw hat drooping,
and worn-out sandals,
dispirited I trace my way home.
At my plain appearance
only a dog barks.
    Even when I return to my snail shell of a hut,

I cannot lie down to sleep.
So at my northern window
I wait up for dawn.
The mindless hoopoe
makes my regret even keener.
Disappointed, all morning
I look at the field.
The farmer's gay songs
are gay no more.
A blind sigh knows no end—
a sigh that knows little of the world.
Only the plow is there,
shining plowshare in the crest,
hung on the wall
of an empty hut,
waiting to work
the thorny field.
   Let's not worry
about the spring plowing.
Long since I have dreamt
of rivers and lakes.
O this unavoidable weakness
of mouth and belly—
so I look at the green bamboo
in the winding waters of Ch'i.[54]
O graceful gentlemen,
lend me a fishing rod.
Among the flowery reeds,
befriending the moon and the fresh breeze,
I'll grow old naturally
among the unsold breeze and unsold moon.
Ingenuous gulls
neither invite nor reject me;
only they won't
start a fight.
   What noble resolve

resides in this clumsy body?
I have given up
several furrows in my field and paddy.
I'll cook gruel if there is rice,
will starve if there is not.
I'll not envy
others and their goods.
You may loathe the poor humble life:
you can't push it away with your hands.
You may envy the rich noble life:
you can't clap your hands to summon it . . .
Everything in life
is ordained.
"To be poor
and still not resent the fact."[55]
Since I have lived thus,
I am happy.
A handful of rice and a gourdful of water
are enough for me.
To be well fed and well clad
is not my dream.
In this world, peaceful and quiet,
let's be loyal and filial,
harmonious with brothers, faithful to friends.
Such a life allows no reproof.
As for other matters,
let them come as they will.

The Hall of Solitary Bliss (1619)
[*Tongnak tang*]

Long ago I heard of Purple Jade Mountain
and the Hall of Solitary Bliss,
those cool and quiet places.
But I was a soldier then,
anxious, with a burning heart.
Danger lurked;[56] our shores were besieged.
Faithful to my duty,
I wielded a glistening spear
and galloped on my armored horse.
But I long for my teacher
even more now that my hair is gray.
Today I start out at last
with bamboo staff and straw sandals.
Like the Wu-i Mountains,[57]
the peaks look graceful,
and the river winds
like the I.
Such a place
needs a host.
Sages and gentlemen
from Silla of a thousand years
and Koryŏ of five hundred,
how many of you have crossed the lovely pass?
Heaven created it; earth has treasured it
and revealed its secrets to him.
Everything has its owner,[58] they say.
How true! Yi Ŏnjŏk is its true owner.
    I push aside tangled creepers
and open the elegant, secluded chamber
of the Hall of Solitary Bliss.
Its beauty is unmatched!
Outside, a thousand stalks of tall bamboo

surround the emerald stream—
and here, ten thousand books
line the walls.
The works of Yen Hui and Master Tseng on the left,
those of Tzu Yu and Tzu Hsia on the right.[59]
He revered the sages of the past[60]
and wrote poems.
In peaceful nature he was so immersed
that he felt at home in all situations.
He called it Solitary Bliss,
a fine name for so elegant a life.
Ssu-ma Kuang had *his* garden of solitary bliss;[61]
but could it match the beauty of this place?
  I enter Truth Nurturing Hermitage
to search for truth.
Winds caress me as I contemplate.
My mind becomes pure and bright:
how marvelous is T'oegye's brush stroke:[62]
I see its matchless excellence.
On my walk to the Fish Viewing Terrace,
the rocks show precious traces
of my teacher's staff and sandals.
The pine he planted retains its ancient air,
how delightful
the unchanging view.
I feel as refreshed as when
I entered his fragrant study.[63]
  I think of the past:
high rocks and sheer cliffs
resemble a mica screen by Lung-mien.[64]
In the lucid mirror of the pool,
the light of the sky and the shadow of clouds entwine,
a cool breeze and bright moonlight
dazzle my eyes.
Hawks and fish[65] were
my teacher's friends.

He contemplated, sought truth,
cultivated learning and virtue.
I cross the stream to a fishing terrace
and ask white gulls near the beach:
birds, do you know
when Yen Kuang returned to the Han House?
The evening smoke settles
on the mossy strand.
    Dressed for spring,
I climb to Yŏnggwi Terrace,
its beauty unchanging throughout the ages;
my spirits are high.
"Enjoy the breeze and go home singing":
today I know the pleasures of Tseng Hsi.
A light rain
over the lotus pond beneath the terrace
scatters pearls
on large jade leaves.
Nature this pure deserves our delight.
How many years have passed
since Chou Tun-i[66] left the world?
Only the perennial fragrance of my teacher
abides!
Through hovering purple mist
a cataract tumbles down
a sheer red cliff—
a long hanging stream.
Where is Incense Burner Peak?
Mount Lu is here.[67]
I look down Lucid Mind Terrace.
My rustic mind cleansed by freshness,
I sit alone
on the terrace,
while the hills are reflected
in the glassy pond with clear breezes.
Birds sing sadly

from green shadows.
I linger and recall
retracing the master's steps.
As always, spring water is crystal clear
at Cap-String–Washing Terrace;
but in the age of decadence
men still struggle in the red dust
when they might be better off
cleaning their cap strings.[68]
   I climb Lion Rock
to view Mount Virtue.
Like jade in its brightness,[69]
my master's brilliance shone here.
Now the phoenix has left, and the hills are bare;[70]
only a solitary cuckoo sighs at dusk.
The spring from Peach Blossom Cave
carries fallen petals day and night.
Is this Mount T'ient'ai?[71] Is it Peach Blossom Spring?
Where is it?
The footsteps of immortals are remote.
I don't know where I am.
I'm not a gentleman
and am far from wise;
but I enjoy the mountain and forget to return home.
Leaning against a rock,
I scan hills and waters
far and near.
Ten thousand flowers
weave a brocade,
and their fragrance
drifts on valley winds.
A distant temple gong
echoes riding the clouds.
Even the pen of Fan Hsi-wen[72]
can't capture this landscape.
So fetching are the views,

they stir the wanderer's heart.
I ramble everywhere
and arrive home late
as the sun sets
behind western hills.
    On my climb again to the Hall of Solitary Bliss
I look about for traces of his presence.
And here he is;
he welcomes me.
"I see him in the soup and on the walls."[73]
Gazing at the sky and ground
I sigh
and recall his deeds.
This is the desk by the window where he sat,
oblivious of worldly cares,
where he read the sages' books
and reaped the fruits of his study.
Thus he continued the tradition, opened a new path,
and brightened the Way for us,
truly a happy gentleman[74] of the east,
the only one worthy of the name.
Further, filial piety and brotherly love as roots,
through loyalty and sincerity,
he became a Hou Chi and Chieh[75]
at the court of the wise king
and hoped to secure
the peace of Yao and Shun.
But the times were adverse,
the loyal and wise were banished.
In high mountains and deep valleys,
those who heard and witnessed lamented.
For seven years
he never saw the sun;
he shut the door to search his mind
and cultivated virtue—the forthright Way.
Right prevailed over evil in the end;

the people acclaimed him of their own accord,
and mindful of
his enduring work,
they erected a shrine in Kanggye,
the place of exile,
remote and poor,
and learned men
hastened to revere him.
  They built an academy on Purple Jade Mountain
above the springs and rocks.
Numerous students
pluck the lute and hum poetry
as though Chou Tun-i and the Loyang scholars[76]
were gathered here once again.
I walk around Goodness Seeking Hall;
it holds the sacred Goodness Embodying Shrine,
where sacrifices to him never cease.
It's not by chance that he is so honored.
  Because we can't
honor him enough,
he's enshrined in the Confucian Temple—
a lovely custom, a grand affair!
Our civilization matches
that of Han, T'ang, and Sung.
Ah, we are in Tzu-yang,
in Cloud Valley.[77]
The water on Sesim Terrace
glows with his virtue and favor.
His spirit lingers
where the dragon reigns.
Wonderful are the workings
of the Heavenly Artificer!
  Overjoyed,
yet unable to fathom
the infinite landscape,
I linger for a month.

I open my rustic mind
to deepen my sincere respect for him
and turn every page
of his works.
His thousand words and myriad sayings
are all wisdom, each revealing
a long tradition and ways of thought
as bright as the sun and moon—
light
illuminating the dark.
    If his thoughts fill our hearts,
if sincere intent directs our minds,[78]
if we order our life to pursue the Way,
if our words are loyal and our deeds faithful,[79]
then goodness will naturally follow.
Ah, let's ponder his teaching,
students,
and look
for myriad years to this wise man,
great as Mount T'ai,[80] remote as the polestar.
Heaven so high and earth so rich,
they, too, will dissolve into dust.
None is eternal but the cool wind that blows
through the Hall of Solitary Bliss.

Song of the Southeast (1635)
[*Yŏngnam ka*]

For a thousand miles along the southern border,
you who survived the invasion,
who first braved the enemy's rage,
what tasks have you now, what work?
In ruins overgrown with weeds

you build a grass roof.
You can't till
stony, barren fields, but
you who have so much to do
are also called to corvée.
Starving, you grow old
in cold and hunger;
but you never forget for a moment
your love for the king.
His royal wisdom, bright as the sun,
extends beyond myriad miles; and
with his deep goodness and lofty virtue,
with love for his subjects,
he sent a special minister
to survey the people,
and we who are spared
see another autumn.
   His intent is clear as white jade
and deep as an ocean:
he felt it his duty
to manifest virtue and renew the people.[81]
With sincere, reverent heart,
abiding in the Nine Standards and Eight Virtues,[82]
he wished to emulate the legendary minister
to serve another Yao and Shun.
He followed the way of former kings
to nurture the people,
taking seventy districts as a family,
and with a mother or father's heart,
looking upon motherless people
as infants,[83]
he bestowed love
sweet as raindrops over the grain crops
in the time of drought,
fresh as water in a pool
to a fish in a dry rut.[84]

His teaching by example reached
myriads upon myriads of houses,
and the spring breeze of rare bounty
blows everywhere.
   His constant favor
is beyond compare.
He urges us to grow grain and mulberry trees
and warns us not to neglect spears and swords.
Man plows, woman weaves;
everyone is at peace and secure.
Bows are strung with arrows[85]
to strengthen our border.
With ice-cold spirit,
with moon-clear breast,
he toiled at affairs of state
and rendered devoted service.
Teaching human relations at school
was the basis of his rule
that serves the Way of Master K'ung—
he thinks this his sole task.
Thus he brightened the Way we tread—
a happy meeting of man and time!
   Deeply moved by
his wise rule,
magistrates of counties
emulate his pattern,
with the same love for people
whether far or near.
Yesterday we bled;[86]
today we live in the Peach Blossom Spring.
Who plucks strings and chants in the halls
covered with pine and bamboo?
Who sings by the willowed arbor,
thumping the ground?
We enjoy golden days of peace[87]
and witness the age of Yao and Shun.

O wretched suitors,
where do you hide?
With no litigation,
the prisons are empty—
the natural result
of change through his teaching.
Now we have no civil suits
after a thousand years.[88]
Offices are in peace,
so are villages.
Men walk on one side,
women on the other.
And in the west land
farmers cede the bank to one another.[89]
Answer, cuckoo,
what is this land?
Ah, have we entered
the kingdom of Chou?[90]
Moved by his rule by example,
let's ask him to stay another year.
 People of the southeast,
hear me.
Let's do one thing
to honor his good work.
Let's buy white silk
and bright colors,
paint his portrait in full figure,
and hang it on the walls
of every house in the southeast,
and when his face flashes through our mind,
we'll see our beloved minister.

Song of the Reedy Stream (1636)
[Nogye ka]

White-haired I visit hills and streams.
I know it's a bit too late,
but in order to meet
my heart's desire,
in the warm spring of the South-Rat year,[91]
putting on my new spring garb,
with bamboo staff and straw sandals,
I visit at just the right moment
the Valley of the Reedy Stream.
Peerless hills and waters
have no owner, unattended,
though recluses and retired scholars frequented them
in older times.
Heaven has secured them, earth has preserved them;
they were meant only for me.
    I hesitate a while
in the setting sun,
climb the high ridge
and view the four corners:
Blue Dragon to the east, White Tiger to the west,
Black Tortoise to the north, Vermilion Bird to the south,[92]
ordered and complete as a painted scroll.
Below the range of hills
to the south,
I advance through thick creepers,
and with a few rafters
build myself a grass roof,
fronting the stream with the hills behind.
Five willows, too, stand before it.[93]
And a cliff one thousand feet high,
like a dragon lurking in the deep,
rims the water's edge;

under the pine crested with passing clouds
my thatched hut
leans on a huge rock.
The displays of nature
are wondrous and strange.
A thousand styles and myriad shapes—
the peaks are graceful
as Mount Fu-ch'un;
waters coil and circle
like Seven-League Shallows;
and, white as snow in April,
miles of fine sand beach.
I'm not Ch'ao-fu or Hsü Yu.
I may not be faithful to my principles,
but here I am by lucky chance,
master of lovely scenes.
Natural the silent green hills and waters,
natural the bright moon and clear breeze;
natural the unsold gulls and herons;
natural, too, many stags and hinds.
The field plowed by Ch'ang-chü and Chieh-ni,[94]
the fishing beach haunted by Yen Kuang,
still unsold, natural, natural!
Since they, too, naturally become mine,
you might say there is another hermit;
I am Yen Kuang,
another Ch'ang-chü or Chieh-ni.
How strange have I become!
Ah, did I become a retired gentlemen
as soon as I entered the hills?
Am I a successor
to an imperishable fragrant name?
Man does not make
his own renown.
The mysteries of the hills and waters
have favored me.

With lustrous mind within,
I cease to think of worldly matters.
The fresh breeze and shining moon
penetrate the bright heart,
and the strong, moving power[95]
renews itself daily.
With birds and beasts
as my cattle,
I fish under the moon
and plow fields among the clouds.
I have little
but I shall not starve.
I can divide among my children
endless hills and waters and idle fields.
But I fear it's hard to allot
a bright moon and clear breeze.
I'd rather choose him who serves my will,[96]
be he gifted or not,
and leave him all
in a certificate drawn by Li Po and T'ao Ch'ien.[97]
You say my words
are ignorant of the world;
but what else have I
for my children but these?
    My way of life has become a habit
to this foolish self,
neither good nor wise.
(It grows stronger as I grow old.)
I would not exchange my waters and hills
for the titles of three dukes.
You may mock my words
as foolish and mad
but you can't
change my life.
What's more in this bright age,
having nothing to do,

I look upon fame and name
as floating clouds
and think only of
happy transcendence,
trusting my life
to hills and waters.
When spring days grow longer,
shouldering a rod,
with a kudzu cap and cotton clothes,
I walk across to the fishing terrace.
Mountain rain has let up,
the sun sends warm rays,
and clear winds come slowly
over the bright surface of the mirror:
I can see black rocks
and count the fishes.
As they know me,
they're not startled;
I can't drop a line to deceive them.
No longer fishing I loiter
and peer down the center of the stream.
The clouds' reflection and the sky's light
entwine and swim,
and fishes leap
above the mirrored clouds.
Startled, I gaze:
above me shines another sky.
A fisherman's flute on a whiff of east wind
rings far above.
How welcoming is this tune
amid quiet river and sky.
Leaning on my staff, facing the wind,
I look left and right—
the clear view on the terrace
is pure and clean.
The water resembles the sky,

the sky, the water.
The blue water and vast sky
are a single color.
Endlessly, white gulls, too,
come and go.
    Mountain flowers by the rocks
weave a brocade,
weeping willows by the water
lower a green veil.
Commanding the fine day
with a beautiful view,
not wanting to squander
this season of flowers,
I summon a boy
and ask him
whether fish and game are to be had
in the deep valleys.
Let's put luscious bracken and scented angelica
between pork and venison,
and place them all
in a large willow box.
Let's taste fresh-minced perch first,
then *nul* fish and pheasant,
set out in colorful array.
And filling a gourd cup
with plain wine from an earthen jug,
drink one by one
until we are drowsy.
And when peach blossoms
shower over our face,
let's prop ourselves up
on a pillow of mossy stone,
welcoming once again
the golden days of peace,
another era of Fu Hsi.

To whom do I owe this life-style?
Royal favor, of course.
Retired as I am among streams and lakes,
how could I forget my king
even for a moment?
Often I raise my eyes
to the polestar,
shedding secret tears
in a corner of the sky.
O heaven,
grant my lifelong wish.
May my holy king enjoy long life
until every hill is made low and every sea runs dry.
In the bright, contented world,
let the sun and moon shine on a peaceful reign,
let swords be sheathed
for a thousand and myriad years,
that people might sing of the blessings of peace
when they work the fields or dig wells,
that this body among hills and waters
might like the winds and moon never age.

SIJO

Early Red Persimmons (1601)
[*Chohongsi ka*]

1

Early red persimmons on the plate;
How beautiful.
They are not pomeloes,
Yet I'll carry them in my pockets.
No one is there to welcome me,
And that makes me sad. [1]

2

I'll catch Wang Hsiang's carp [2]
And gather Meng Tsung's bamboo shoots. [3]
Until my hair turns white,
I'll wear Lao Lai Tzu's clothes
And all my life, like Master Tseng, [4]
Serve my parents' every wish.

3

I'll stretch thirty thousand pounds of iron
And braid an ever-longer rope.
And in the ninety thousand leagues of heaven,
I'll tie the moving sun down:
May my gray-haired parents
Age slowly.

4

When a crow joins
A flock of phoenix,
It's like a single rock
In a pile of white jade.
Enough! Phoenix too are birds.
Why not mingle with them and play?

Pepper Well (1619)
[*Sukchŏng*]

5

Does the Pepper Well hide
Some medicine unknown to the Divine Husbandman?[5]
I soak myself in the water
Where the autumn sun shines.
Today I feel like Tseng Hsi,[6]
Who performed lustration in the River I.

6

With no ambition in the red dust,
I set my heart on Confucian culture.
Continuing the past, opening the future,
He illuminates our path.
Oh, I have seen Master Chu again[7]
After a thousand years.

Twenty-nine Songs on the Standing Rock (1629)
[*Ibam isipku kok*]

7

Unfeeling rock standing here,
You seem so welcoming!
Even men, lords of creation,
Find it hard to stand firm.
Having stood alone from times past,
You have never changed your stance.

8

It towers at the river's mouth;
The higher I gaze upward, the higher it soars.
It is unchanging in the wind and frost;
The deeper I bore, the harder it becomes.[8]
If a man were like this rock,
He would be a great hero!

9

I cannot get to know you,
O wordless rock.
But I am here to admire
Your noble form and upright bearing.
The world does not know
How to make three beneficial friends.[9]

10

You were not drawn with a plumb line—
How could you know the compass and square?[10]
Lofty and straight,
So noble you appear.
Ah, can we fall short of you,
We who are known as men?

11

You stand loftily erect,
Worthy of emulation.
In a gorge covered with clouds,
Who will seek you?
Only one who stirs himself to climb
Will discover many novel sights.

12

"Man's ways being so strange,
Are you pleased to see me?
Lowering myself to rely on others,[11]
Whither might I climb?
I will grow old as I am,
Here where the mountains and rivers are good."

13

From the time of the Heavenly Emperor,
How many have delighted in seeing you
Alone in the deep mountains?
How many have passed by?
Tell me, please,
Of the many heroes of the past.

14

"After Ch'ao-fu and Hsü Yu,
I met Hermit Yen Kuang.[12]
After he had departed,
No one knew my worth.
Today again I meet you,
Lucky, indeed, these times."

15

Let me ask you again quietly
How many thousands of years old you are.
You age is surely great,
And mine small.
Now let us grow old together,
You and I.

16

"Was it two days ago, the age of Yao and Shun?
Was it yesterday, the ages of Han, T'ang, and Sung?
Time flows like a dream;
How many years have been allotted me?
I, too, will grow old with you
Before the fifth millennium is over".[13]

17

With my small thatched hut
Set among boulders,
My feeble eyes are used to
The colors of bamboo and pine.
Here I cannot tell
When spring goes and autumn comes.

18

I'm told that Confucius said,
"It is Shang who bears me up."[14]
Today the one who bears me up
Is this mute rock.
My foolish, base, and cluttered mind
Is renewed of its own accord.

19

I have climbed Kyegu Terrace;
Suddenly I tremble and grow wary.[15]
Merely looking about me
Makes me so afraid.
How could I not be careful
At a place unseen and unheard of?

20

The moon rising from a peak
Shines down from among the mountains.
The ninety-thousand-league heavens
Are so far and so high.
This lofty peak pierces them
That seem to float above it.

21

High, high, Nine Fathom Peak
Beautiful among the mountains!
The studies of men here below[16]
Are as numerous as these peaks.
But why did the Maker stop short
With a basket of earth?[17]

22

Who called it South Lu Peak?
Was it on this East Mountain
That Confucius said Lu was small?[18]
You have been green for aeons
And tall;
Yet you do not know where you are.

23

Aloof from fame and fortune,
With hempen clothes and a staff,
I seek mountains and rivers
And enter P'ise Terrace.
Ah, here indeed is
Peach Blossom Spring!

24

The swiftly falling waters at Hamnyu Terrace
Seem to play tricks.
Flowing this way or that,
They come together from left and right.
Now I know they will find the source
Even when split into separate streams.[19]

25

Waters rushing to Simjin Grotto
Meander about beneath the rock.
Flowing day and night,
They meet before the pavilion.
Ah, it is like viewing again
The Lo and I rivers.[20]

26

Children under the pine tree,
Where are your parents?
"They have gone to gather magic herbs,
And it is time for them to return.
With the clouds thick over the mountains,
We do not know where they are now."

27

In the crystal waters of Yokhak Pool
I bathe with a crane.
After following blossoms and willows
I return home elated.
I do not envy Tseng Hsi, who took the air
At the Rain Dance altars and came back singing.

28

The pool's water is crystal clear;
I see all the fish that pass.
One, two, three, four—
I can count them all.
Boy, try once more to count them
As they leap from the clear water.

29

Napping on the strand,
I awake when the moon is bright.
With my goosefoot staff aslant
I cross Rolling Jade Bridge.
Only the drowsing birds hear
The stream's clear music.

30

With my fishing pole aslant
I wend my way along Chowŏl Rapids.
Parting red smartweed,
I sit beneath the moon.
I do not envy the pleasures
Of Yen Kuang on the T'ung River.

31

The fields that Ch'ang-chü and Chieh-ni tilled
Have lain fallow a thousand years.
I push aside the clouds
And plow two or three rows.
I would not call my life one of plenty,
But I have nothing to envy.

32

I gaze at Chŏngun Peak,
So vivid in the heavens.
If I ascended that rocky hill,
I could view the five-hued clouds of fairyland.
But tears well up in my feeble eyes
And dim my sight.

33

I climb Sanji Peak,
My whole body exuding fragrance.
Mount Shang of the Four Whiteheads[21]
Was here as well, perhaps.
But so thick are the clouds
I cannot tell what place this is.

34

Kyŏkchin Peak is so high
That even the red dust is distant.
The more I clean my deaf ears,
The deafer they become.
Beyond the mountains I cannot hear or see
The difference between right and wrong.

35

On a broad field beneath the pines
At the range's end, following the river,
Azure mists and a crimson glow
Bathe the mountains, fold upon fold.
Ah, it is as beautiful
As a freshly painted mica screen!

Songs of the Five Relations (after 1634)
[*Oryun ka*]

36

My father begot me;
My mother reared me:
How hard it is to repay their kindness,
Boundless as heaven.
Great Shun's lifelong devotion
Was not enough, it seems.[22]

37

In the hundred years of a man's life
There are illnesses of many kinds.
So for how many years
Can we serve our parents?
I will discharge my filial duties
By doing all I can in this life.

38

I will serve my parents
With utmost sincerity,
Rising at cockcrow, washing myself
And asking if they are too warm or too cold.
Every day I will be at their side
Serving selflessly without rest.

39

O people of the world,
Do you know the love of a parent?
Were it not for my parents,
Would this body exist?
Serve them with ritual from start to finish
During their lives and after their deaths.[23]

40

Among the three thousand sins
The worst is unfilial behavior.
Take the words of Master K'ung
As the great, unchanging norm.
I will teach this truth
Even to the very dullest.

41

Do you know
How boundless is royal favor?
Were it not for this,
How could the myriad people live?
Would that I could repay
The magnanimity of my king.

42

How boundless is the royal favor
Though I'm not a wise minister![24]
Even were to I die a hundred times
I could not repay it all.
Because men fuss about success and failure,
I cannot serve him, and so I grieve.

43

Men are born to serve
King and father together;
They are one,
Ponder not their relative worth.
Between loyalty and filial devotion,
I know not how to grow old.

44

Night comes to the deep mountains;
The north wind grows colder.
Does this wind blow
Through the Jade Tower?
I gaze at the polestar and pray:
May he be warm throughout this long night.

45

After my death
My loyal self will become a spirit
Flying up higher and higher,
Opening the gate of heaven,[25]
And imploring the Jade Emperor:
May he grant long life to our king!

46

After husband and wife
Come father and son, older and younger brothers.
Were it not for man and wife,
How could the Five Relations exist?
For thus men came into being,
Exalting the bond of man and wife.

47

When heaven begot men,
Marriage thus began.
Heaven fixed worthy matches,
Important are man and wife.
Making a morning of your life
And harmonize like small and large zithers together.[26]

48

What counts between man and wife
Is not just companionship.
Live within ritual norms
And respect one another.
Treat each other like guests
Throughout your lives, as would Hsi Chi.[27]

49

Man and wife—
How grave they are.
The husband calls, the wife follows;
Then the family is in harmony.
Respect and serve your husband
Like Meng Kuang of the Later Han.[28]

50

Though born as strangers,
How important are man and wife!
The hundred blessings of mankind
Are found in marriage.
Such being the ties,
How can harmony be lacking?

51

When brothers are born,
They grow from the same stem.
How precious they are,
Of the same flesh and blood.
Love your brothers as one with your body
Your whole life through.

52

To quarrel over an estate is to lose one's nature.
Cause no discord among brothers.
You may buy paddies and fields,
Even male and female slaves.
But can you buy a brother
At any price?

53

Love your brothers dearly
And live together for a hundred years.
Share one set of clothes
And one bowl of rice.
Grow so old your hair turns white,
And you cannot recognize one another.

54

The three of us once lived
As a single body.
Where did the two younger ones go,
Forgetting to return?
At every sunset outside the gate
I cannot restrain a sigh.[29]

55

Deep brotherly love has
No inside and no outside.
I thought we had achieved
Perfect harmony in brotherhood.
Who knew that I would be a stray goose,
Old and crying alone?

56

Be faithful
In dealings with your friends.
Can one see his friends
Without respecting them?
Throughout your life
Maintain careful courtesy.

57

While faithful in speech and sincere in action,
Be circumspect in making friends.
Then there will be no disgrace,
And few will blame you.
If you are careless in friendship
You will disgrace your own parents.

58

Between heaven and earth,
Man is the noblest creature.
What we must cherish are
The Five Relations.
If man did not know these,
He would resemble the birds and beasts.

59

Luckily throughout the ages
People clung to customs and norms.
Thus have I gathered what I have heard
And compiled a few poems.
Take pains, O my juniors,
To examine and practice them!

60

Who, if he inspected these poems,
Would not be inspired?
My writing may be clumsy,
But it is filled with sincerity and seriousness.
Scan my poems and savor them;
Then you will need no other aid.

Thinking of Parents and Other Poems (c. 1636)

Thinking of Parents
[*Sach'in*]

61

Frost and dew;
It hurts me to tread on them,
Though not because my clothes are threadbare
Or because I fear the cold.
One square inch of boundless longing
Suddenly moves me to tears.

Longing for the Worthy
[*Mohyŏn*]

62

Oh, joy! In a dream I saw
The sages Po I and Shu Ch'i.
Solemnly, and with shifting colors,
They spoke:
"Even now, we cherish loyalty
As when we reined in the horse of King Wu."[30]

63

The waters of Milo River
Are the bitter tears of Ch'ü Yüan.
Even a spirit could not forget
His loyalty and indignation.
The sound of sobbing waters:
Was it yesterday he drowned himself here?

Secluded Life at Reed Islet
[*Noju yugŏ*]

64

O children, discard your worldly cares
And let us go.
The field and gardens are empty,
So let us set out.
The bright moon and clear breeze on the To River³¹
Have long awaited me.

Admonishing Myself
[*Chagyŏng*]

65

Children and adults know
That we must polish
The bright mirror crusted with dirt
Even if we must pay for the cleaning.
But men don't know how to cultivate
Bright virtue, though it can be polished for free.

66

I view the Gate of the Eight Virtues³²
Beyond the Pass of Sincerity:
There is one great avenue,
So broad and straight!
Why is it that all day long
None come or go there?

67

I will cut down a tall pine on Mount Kuin
And make a Boat of Worldwide Salvation
To ferry across all those
Who have lost their way.
But a boatman, too, is foolish—
He abandons his boat on a sunset beach.

*

68

Fish sporting in rivers and lakes—
Do not boast of your luck.
After the fisherman has gone,
White gulls will spy on you.
Floating and diving the whole day through,
You have no time for rest.

Yun Sŏndo

1587 Born in eastern Seoul as the second son of Yun Yusim (27 July)
1597 Studies at a mountain monastery
1604 Marries a daughter of Yun Ton
1612 Obtains the "Literary Licentiate" degree
1616 Over his father's objections, submits a memorial censuring a powerful and corrupt minister
1617 Sent into exile to Kyŏngwŏn (second month)
1623 Released and returned to Haenam (third month)
1628 Passes the special examination; appointed tutor to the heir apparent (later King Hyojong)
1633 Passes another examination; Fourth Minister of Rites and Fourth Inspector
1635 Demoted because of court intrigue
1637 Reaches Kanghwa Island (23 February) to serve King Injo in his temporary headquarters; on his way home finds a beautiful spot for his retreat and names it Lotus Grotto
1638 Recalled to the capital but refuses; his enemies make it an issue and transport him to Yŏngdŏk
1639 Released in the second month; retreats to Crystal Grotto and Flute Listening Grotto
1642 Writes "New Songs in the Mountain" in Grotto of Golden Chains
1645 Writes "More New Songs in the Mountain" and other poems in Grotto of Golden Chains
1651 Opponents scheme to prevent his recall by King Hyojong, his erstwhile pupil; retires to Lotus Grotto and writes "The Angler's Calendar"
1652 Returns to the capital at the special summons from the king; appointed Sixth Royal Secretary, but falls ill and retires to Yangju where he writes his last three poems

1653– Moves back and forth between the two grottoes
1657
1657 Appointed Fifth Minister without portfolio (eleventh month)
1658 Dismissed because of factionalism (10 September)
1660 Issue over such ritual questions as the length of mourning for
   Hyojong's Queen Mother; the Westerners, the poet's political
   enemies, banish him to Samsu
1667 Released from exile (seventh month)
1671 Dies in Lotus Grotto (16 July); buried in Flute Listening Grotto
   (4 October)
1675 King Sukchong accords him the posthumous rank of Minister of
   Personnel

Dispelling Gloom (1618)
[*Kyŏnhoe yo*]

1

Whether sad or joyful,
Whether right or wrong,
I'll order and polish
Only my duty and the Way.
In other matters,
I'll not discriminate.

2

I myself know that sometimes
I was absurd and missed the mark.
My mind was foolish but
I only desired to honor you.
Beware, my lord, and reflect on
The words of those slanderers.

3

O stream that flows sobbing
Past South Gate Tower.[1]
For what reasons, moving water,
Do you flow night and day?
You follow my crimson heart
And thus run on and on.

4

A chain of mountains is long, long;
Waters flow far, far.
Love for parents is endless,
And my heart is heavy.
Faroff, crying sadly,
A lone wild goose flies by.

5

I have borne from the beginning
Vast love for parents
And a loyal heart for the lord;
Heaven has fashioned it thus.
To forget one's lord
Is to be unfilial to one's parents.

After the Rain (1617)
[*Uhu yo*]

6

Has the dreary rain ceased?
Have the dark clouds rolled away?
The deep swamps in the stream in front,
You say, now are limpid.
Come then; if the water is truly clear,
Let me wash my cap strings.[2]

New Songs in the Mountain (1642)
[*Sanjung singok*]

Random Thoughts
[*Manhŭng*]

7

Among mountains and streams I build
A thatched hut under the rock.
The ignorant mock my grass roof;
Can they fathom my true intent?
Indeed, this life best befits
A simple but rustic mind.[3]

8

Cooked barley and fresh herbs—
I have had a fair amount of these.
And by the rock in the stream
I play to my heart's content.
What further need have I?
I long for nothing, nothing else.

9

Alone, cup in hand,
I view distant peaks.
Even if my love came to me,
Would I be happier?
Mountains neither speak nor smile,
But what happiness, what joy.

10

Some say my life rivals the three dukes';
Even a mighty ruler cannot match it.
I ponder the matter—
Ch'ao-fu and Hsü Yu were indeed pure.[4]
Nothing can match my idle pleasures
Among trees and springs.

11

Heaven, too, has learned my secret:
I am by nature slow.
Hence among all in life
It has left me not a thing.
Heaven appoints me guardian
Of peaceful hills and waters.

12

You say that the hills and waters are good,
But can I enjoy them all?
Now I know better
The vast favor of my lord.
Can I return his love,
Even its smallest part?

Morning Mist
[*Chomu yo*]

13

East Mountain[5] was lofty,
But how jealous is the morning mist.
It hides for a while
The majestic first peak.
Yet the mist will soon vanish
As the sun's bright rays dispel it.

Summer Rain
[*Hau yo*]

14

Go not to the field when it rains;
Close the twig gate and feed the cattle.
A tiresome rain comes only once,
So polish now your plows and hoes.
Rest until the day clears;
Then we'll plow the long furrow.

15

How dull is the dreary rain,
Yet only in the rainy season am I idle.
How gloomy is the darkness,
Yet only at night have I leisure.
Sleep early, boy,
And get up when the east reddens.

Sunset
[*Ilmo yo*]

16

The mountains are more beautiful
After the sun has crossed them.
It is twilight:
Darkness settles.
Watch out for tigers now, boy;
Do not wander about in the fields.

Deep Night
[*Yasim yo*]

17

Close the paper screen; the wind is rising.
Blow out the candles; night is deepening.
Let us rest on pillows
And sleep the night through.
Boy, wake me when the sky
Is filled with dawn.

Lament on the Lean Year
[*Kise t'an*]

18

You accuse me of doing wrong
By borrowing grain from the Office.[6]
Po I and Shu Ch'i gathered ferns;[7]
I know all about their rectitude.
But do not blame me:
The harvest was bad this year.

Songs of Five Friends
[*Ou ka*]

19

How many friends have I? Count them:
Water and stone, pine and bamboo—
The rising moon on the east mountain,
Welcome, it too is my friend.
What need is there, I say,
To have more friends than five?

20

They say the color of clouds is fine,
But they often darken.
They say the sound of winds is clear,
But they often cease to blow.
It is only the *water,* then,
That is perpetual and good.

21

Why do flowers fade so soon
Once they are in their glory?
Why do grasses yellow so soon
Once they have grown tall?
Perhaps it is the *stone,* then,
That is constant and good.

22

Flowers bloom when it is warm;
Leaves fall when the days are cool.
But, O *pine,* how is it
That you scorn frost, ignore snow?
I know now even your roots are
Straight among the Nine Springs. [8]

23

You are not a tree,
Nor are you a plant.
Who let you shoot up so straight?
What makes you empty within?
You are green in all seasons,
Welcome, *bamboo,* my friend.

24

Small but floating high,
You shed light on all creation.
And what can match your brightness
In the dark of night?
You look at me but with no words;
That's why, O *moon,* you are my friend.

More New Songs in the Mountain (1645)
[*Sanjung sok singok*]

Autumn Night
[*Ch'uya cho*]

25

Now that the flies[9] are all gone,
You don't need a fly trap any more.
Now that fallen leaves sough in the wind,
Wrinkles will devour my lord.
The moon is my friend—
It shines among bamboo groves.

Spring Dawn
[*Ch'unhyo ŭm*]

26

A hard winter is over—
Where are the bitter winds now?
Spring trails over distant hills,
The mild air is still.
I will open a paper screen
To admire the sky dyed by dawn.

To an Old Zither
[*Kogŭm yŏng*]

27

I take out an abandoned zither,
Change the strings and play
An elegant tune of the past,
The same refined sound.
But who else knows the tune I played?
I have to put it back in the case.

To My Friend[10]
[*Chŭng Pangŭm*]

28

Heart wants to sing, but cannot sing alone;
Heart wants to dance, but dancing must have music.
  Then lute shall play,
For none but lute can strike the secret tone
    My heart would sing
    So heart and song are one;
    Then lute shall play,
For none but lute knows what is heart's desire
    So heart may spring
    Into dance
    And tap out its rhythm.
Welcome, sweet lute, my dear, dearest friend,
There is no hurt your music cannot mend.

At the Beginning of the Feast
[*Ch'oyŏn kok*]

29

Do you know how a house is built?
It is the work of an artisan.
Do you know why wood is straight?
It is planed so by the plumb line.[11]
If you know this truth of your house,
You will then enjoy a long life.

30

Do you know why the wine is good?
It is so through the work of yeast.
Do you know why broth is delicious?
It is so through salt and prunes.[12]
If you know this truth about food,
You will then enjoy a long life.

At the End of the Feast
[*P'ayŏn kok*]

31

You may relax and be happy;
But should you forget your cares?
You may play and be merry;
But is it not hard to play on and on?
If you know these cares,
You will then enjoy a long life.

32

You may drink wine;
But without virtue, disorder will ensue.[13]
You may dance to music;
But without decorum, confusion will arise.
If you keep virtue and decorum,
You will then enjoy a long life.

The Angler's Calendar (1651)
[*Ŏbu sasi sa*]

Spring

33

Fog lifts in the stream before me,
The sun lances the back hills.
Cast off, cast off!
The night tide neaps, and now
High water rushes upon the shore.
Chigukch'ong chigukch'ong ŏsawa.
Flowers in river hamlets are fair to see,
But distant views swell my heart.

34

Day is warm,
Fishes float in the blue.
Hoist anchor, hoist anchor!
In twos or threes,
Gulls come and go.
Chigukch'ong chigukch'ong ŏsawa.
Boy, I have a rod;
Have you loaded a flagon of wine?

35

A puff of east wind ruffles
The stream's surface into ripples.
Raise sail, raise sail!
Let's go to West Lake
By the East.
Chigukch'ong chigukch'ong ŏsawa.
Hills pass by,
More hills greet us.

36

Is it a cuckoo that cries?
Is it the willow that is blue?
Row away, row away!
Several roofs in a far fishing village
Swim in the mist.
Chigukch'ong chigukch'ong ŏsawa.
Boy, fetch an old net!
Fishes are climbing against the stream.[14]

37

The sun's fair rays are shining,
Water shimmers like oil.
Row away, row away!
Should we cast a net,
Or drop a line on such a day?
Chigukch'ong chigukch'ong ŏsawa.
The Fisherman's Song stirs my fancy;[15]
I have forgotten all about fishing.

38

Let's return to the shore,
Twilight trails in the west.
Lower sail, lower sail!
How supple and sweet
Willows and flowers on the riverbank!
Chigukch'ong chigukch'ong ŏsawa.
Who would envy three dukes?
Who would now think of earthy affairs?

39

Let's tread on fragrant grasses
And pick orchids and angelica.
Stop the boat, stop the boat!
What have I taken aboard
On my boat small as a leaf?
Chigukch'ong chigukch'ong ŏsawa.
Nothing except mist when I set sail,
When I row back, the moon is my tenant.

40

Drunk I lie asleep,
What if the boat floats downstream?
Moor the boat, moor the boat!
Peach Blossom Spring is near,
Pink petals leap on the stream.
Chigukch'ong chigukch'ong ŏsawa.
I am far away from red dust—
The world of men.

41

Let's stop angling and see
The moon through the bamboo awning.
Drop anchor, drop anchor!
Night settles,
The cuckoo sings a sweet song.
Chigukch'ong chigukch'ong ŏsawa.
The heart shouts its peak of joy,
I have lost my way in the dark.

42

Tomorrow, tomorrow, we have tomorrow.
A spring night will soon see the day.
Bring the boat ashore, bring the boat ashore!
With rod for a cane,
Let's find our twig gate.
Chigukch'ong chigukch'ong ŏsawa.
This angler's life is
How I shall pass my days.

Summer

43

Tedious rain over at last,
The stream grows limpid.
Cast off, cast off!
Rod on my shoulder,
I can't still my loud heart.
Chigukch'ong chigukch'ong ŏsawa.
Who has painted these scenes,
Misty rivers and folded peaks?

44

Wrap the steamed rice in lotus leaves,
You need no other viands.
Hoist anchor, hoist anchor!
I've already got my blue arum hat,
Bring me, boy, my green straw cape.
Chigukch'ong chigukch'ong ŏsawa.
Mindless gulls come and go;
Do they follow me, or I them?

45

A wind rises among the water chestnut,
Cool is the bamboo awning.
Raise sail, raise sail!
Let the boat drift with the current,
The summer breeze is capricious.
Chigukch'ong chigukch'ong ŏsawa.
Northern coves and southern river,
Does it matter where I go?

46

When the river is muddy,
No matter if we wash our feet there.
Row away, row away!
I wish to go the Wu River; sad
Are the angry waves of a thousand years.[16]
Chigukch'ong chigukch'ong ŏsawa.
Paddle the boat, then, to the Ch'u River;[17]
But don't catch the fish of a loyal soul.

47

How rare is a mossy jetty
With willow groves, thick and green.
Row away, row away!
Remember when we reach the fishing rock,
Anglers don't fight for the best pool.
Chigukch'ong chigukch'ong ŏsawa.
When you meet a hoary hermit,
Yield him the choicest stream.[18]

48

Whelmed by my exalted mood,
I had not known day was ending.
Lower sail, lower sail!
Let's beat the stroke
With a song of roving waves.
Chigukch'ong chigukch'ong ŏsawa.
Who can know how my heart
Always delights in the creak of an oar?

49

The setting sun is splendid.
Twilight will soon overtake us!
Stop the boat, stop the boat!
Under the pine a path
Winds through the rocks.
Chigukch'ong chigukch'ong ŏsawa.
Do you hear an oriole calling
Here and there in the green grove?

50

Let's spread our net out on the sand
And lie under the thatched awning.
Moor the boat, moor the boat!
Fan off mosquitoes,
No, flies are worse.
Chigukch'ong chigukch'ong ŏsawa.
Only one worry, even here,
Traitors[19] might eavesdrop.

51

What will the mood of the sky be?
Winds and storm may rise at night.
Drop anchor, drop anchor!
Who said that a boat swings by itself
At the ferry landing?[20]
Chigukch'ong chigukch'ong ŏsawa.
Lovely are the hidden plants
Growing along mountain torrents.

52

Look! My snail-shell hut
With white clouds all around.
Bring the boat ashore, bring the boat ashore!
Let's climb the stone path
With bulrush fan in hand.
Chigukch'ong chigukch'ong ŏsawa.
O idle life of an old angler,
This is my work, this is my life.

Autumn

53

What is more transcendent
Than the life of a complete angler?
Cast off, cast off!
Mock not a hoary fisherman,
He's painted by every great hand.
Chigukch'ong chigukch'ong ŏsawa.
Are the joys of all seasons equal?
No, autumn has most delights.

54

Autumn comes to a river village,
The fishes are many and sleek.
Hoist anchor, hoist anchor!
Let's be free and happy
On myriad acres of limpid waves.
Chigukch'ong chigukch'ong ŏsawa.
Behind me the dusty world, but
Joy doubles as farther I sail away.

55

Where white clouds rise,
Branches rustle.
Raise sail, raise sail!
Let's go to West Lake at high tide,
And at low water to East Lake.
Chigukch'ong chigukch'ong ŏsawa.
White clover ferns and pink knotweeds,
They adorn every inlet.

56

Beyond where the wild geese fly
Unknown peaks emerge.
Row away, row away!
I'll angle there, of course, but
My zestful spirit is enough.
Chigukch'ong chigukch'ong ŏsawa.
As the setting sun shines,
A thousand hills are brocade.

57

Silver scales and jade scales,
Did I have a good catch today?
Row away, row away!
Let's build a fire of reed bushes,
Broil the fishes one by one.
Chigukch'ong chigukch'ong ŏsawa.
Pour wine from a crock jar
Filling up my gourd cup!

58

Gently, the side wind blowing,
We return with sail lowered.
Lower sail, lower sail!
Darkness is overcoming the day,
But clear delight lingers.
Chigukch'ong chigukch'ong ŏsawa.
Who can tire of
The red trees and crystal waters?

59

A scatter of silver dews;
The bright moon rises.
Stop the boat, stop the boat!
Far and foggy is the Phoenix Tower,[21]
To whom should I give this clear light?
Chigukch'ong chigukch'ong ŏsawa.
The jade hare pounds the magic pills;
Would I could feed them to heroes.

60

Where is it, where am I?
Are heaven and earth separate?
Moor the boat, moor the boat!
Since the west wind's dust can't reach us,
Why fan off the empty air?[22]
Chigukch'ong chigukch'ong ŏsawa.
Further, since I have heard no words,
Why should I bother to wash my ears?

61

Frost falls on my clothes:
I am not cold.
Drop anchor, drop anchor!
Don't complain that the boat is narrow;
Compare it instead to the floating world.
Chigukch'ong chigukch'ong ŏsawa.
We'll live this way
Tomorrow and ever.

62

I want to admire the dawn moon
From a stone cave in the pine grove.
Bring the boat ashore, bring the boat ashore!
But the path in the empty hills
Is hidden by fallen leaves.
Chigukch'ong chigukch'ong ŏsawa.
Since the white clouds, too, follow me,
O heavy is the sedge cape!

Winter

63

The clouds have rolled away,
The sun's rays are warm.
Cast off, cast off!
Heaven and earth are frozen hard,
But water as always is clear and cold.
Chigukch'ong chigukch'ong ŏsawa.
The boundless water
Is silk brocade.

64

Mend your fishing line and rod,
Repair the boat with bamboo sheets.
Hoist anchor, hoist anchor!
They say the nets on the Hsiao and Hsiang
And the Tungt'ing Lake freeze.[23]
Chigukch'ong chigukch'ong ŏsawa.
At this time no place is
Better than our waters.

65

Fishes in the shallows
Are gone to distant swamps.
Raise sail, raise sail!
The sun shines for a moment;
So let's go out to the fishing place.
Chigukch'ong chigukch'ong ŏsawa.
If the bait is good,
Fat fishes will bite, they say.

66

A snow settles over the night—
What new scenes before my eyes!
Row away, row away!
In front lie glassy acres,
Jade hills piled behind.
Chigukch'ong chigukch'ong ŏsawa.
Is it a fairy land, or Buddha's realm?
It can't be the world of man.

67

I've forgotten the net and rod
And beat the side of the boat.
Row away, row away!
How many times have I wished
To cross the stream ahead?
Chigukch'ong chigukch'ong ŏsawa.
What if a gale should rise
And set my boat in motion?

68

The crows hastening to their nests,
How many have flown overhead?
Lower sail, lower sail!
Darkness envelopes our homeward path,
Evening snow lies thick.
Chigukch'ong chigukch'ong ŏsawa.
Who'll attack Oya Lake[24]
And avenge the shame of soldier trees?[25]

69

Red cliffs and emerald canyons
Enfold us like a painted screen.
Stop the boat, stop the boat!
What does it matter
If I catch any fish or not?[26]
Chigukch'ong chigukch'ong ŏsawa.
In an empty boat, with straw cape and hat,
I sit and my heart beats fast.

70

By the river a lone pine,
How mighty, how towering.
Moor the boat, moor the boat!
Don't scorn the rough clouds—
They screen the world from us.
Chigukch'ong chigukch'ong ŏsawa.
Don't deplore the roaring waves—
They drown out the clamor of this world.

71

People have praised my way of life
In the land of the hermits.
Drop anchor, drop anchor!
Tell me who wore
The sheepskin cloth at Seven-League Shallows?[27]
Chigukch'ong chigukch'ong ŏsawa.
And for three thousand six hundred days
Let's count the time on our fingers.[28]

72

Day closes,
Time to feast and rest.
Bring the boat ashore, bring the boat ashore!
Let's tread the path where snow
Is strewn with pink petals.
Chigukch'ong chigukch'ong ŏsawa.
Lean from the pine window and gaze
As the snow moon crosses the western peak.

The Disappointing Journey (1652)
[*Mongch'ŏn yo*]

73

Am I awake? Am I asleep?
I ascend to a city of white jade.
The Jade Emperor welcomes me,
But a host of spirits envy my presence.
Forgo them all; my only joys are
The five lakes and a hazy moon.

74

I dream a dream in fitful sleep
And enter the Palace of Twelve Towers.
The Jade Emperor smiles at me,
But a host of spirits revile me.
When then can I ask
About the billion people on earth?

75

When heaven is torn to rags,
What art can stitch it together?
When the White Jade Tower falls,
Which artisan can raise it up?
I cannot appeal to the Jade Emperor;
I return with lips sealed.

NOTES

ABBREVIATIONS

CKK   Chōsen kosho kankōkai edition
KSYB *Kosan sŏnsaeng yŏnbo*
SPPY Ssu-pu pei-yao edition
SPTK Ssu-pu ts'ung-k'an edition
SPY   *Songgang pyŏlchip, yŏnbo*

INTRODUCTION

1. See my *Songs of Flying Dragons: A Critical Reading* (Cambridge: Harvard University Press, 1975), pp. 84–85.

2. The local agency *(hyangch'ŏng)* was "organized in each county by its *yangban* residents and through it they wielded considerable influence. This office undertook responsibility for assisting the magistrate, rectifying public mores, and scrutinizing the county's petty functionaries." See Ki-baik Lee, *A New History of Korea,* trans. Edward W. Wagner with Edward J. Shultz (Seoul: Ilchogak, 1984), pp. 176–178. For the village compact *(hyangyak)* and private academy *(sŏwŏn),* see Lee, pp. 205–208 and 206–208, respectively.

3. In debates on the relative importance of the classics and literature, those favoring scriptural scholarship argued that students read only selections of poetry and prose in anthologies and neglected the classics. Those favoring literary composition retorted that a one-sided emphasis on the classics would produce few writers who could serve as diplomats, write and harmonize with Chinese hosts in China, or entertain Chinese envoys to Korea. Some militant reformists—those implicated in the 1519 purge, especially Cho Kwangjo (1482–1519)—asserted that the sovereign should not compose poetry and should not command his officials to present poems to him. In practice, however, most scholar-officials, including Neo-Confucian philosophers, studied both the classics and literature, as their collected works seem to testify.

4. Lee, *New History of Korea,* pp. 204–206.

5. Ibid., pp. 208–209.

6. A reply to a memorial submitted by No Susin (1515–1590). See SPY, 2A.23a–b.

7. SPY, 3B.30b, 36b, 39a.

8. Ibid., 3B.49b–50a; *Sŏnjo sujŏng sillok,* 26.8a–b.

9. *Songgang pyŏlchip,* 4.207.

10. Yi I, *Kyŏngyŏn ilgi,* 3.86a, in *Yulgok chŏnsŏ* (Taedong munhwa yŏnguwŏn ed., 1958). In their prefaces to *The Works,* Sin Hŭm (1566–1628) and Yi Chŏnggwi (1564–1635) mention "intolerance" (pp. 5–6).

11. Yun's memorial denounced Minister of Rites Yi Ich'ŏm (1560–1623) as corrupt. See *Kwanghaegun ilgi,* T'aebaeksan ed., 110.98 ff.; Chŏngjoksan ed., 110.8b–14b; *KSYB,* 1.3a–5b; *Kosan yugo,* 6.2b–3a.

12. *KSYB,* 1.16a; *Kosan yugo,* 6.8b–9a, 9a–b.

13. *KSYB,* 1.13a.

14. Ibid., 1.21a–22a; *Kosan yugo,* 6.11b–12a.

15. *KSYB,* 1.25a–27b; *Kosan yugo,* 6.13b–15a. Later King Chŏngjo (r. 1777–1800) praised Yun's expert opinion and ordered his memorial to be included in his collected works (*Chŏngjo sillok,* 52.57b–58a).

16. Yun's memorial in support of a three-year mourning period was submitted on 26 May 1660; on 2 June his memorial was burnt and he was banished to Samsu, South Hamgyŏng. See *Hyŏngjong sillok,* 2.27b–31b; *KSYB,* 2.28b–31b; *Kosan yugo,* 6.15a–b.

17. *Hyŏnjong sillok,* 2.43a; *Kosan yugo,* 6.15b.

18. *KSYB,* 3.6b.

19. *Songgang pyŏlchip,* pp. 408–415.

20. Ch'a Ch'ŏlla (1556–1615), *Osan sŏllim* (CKK, 1909), 111.

21. Cyril Birch, ed., *Anthology of Chinese Literature: From Early Times to the Fourteenth Century* (New York: Grove Press, 1965), p. 209.

22. Ch'a Ch'ŏlla, *Osan sŏllim,* 95.

23. Sŏ Kŏjŏng (1420–1488), *P'irwŏn chapki* (CKK, 1909), 2.65; Yi Yuk (1438–1504), *Ch'ŏngp'a kŭktam* (CKK, 1909), 85.

24. Sŏng Hyŏn (1439–1504), *Yongjae ch'onghwa* (CKK, 1909), 3.19.

25. Cho Sin (fl. 1479), *Somun swaerok* (CKK, 1909), 6.

26. James A. Notopoulos, "Mnemosyne in Oral Literature," *Transactions of the American Philological Association* 69 (1938): 491. Also relevant is Stephen Owen, *Remembrances: The Experience of the Past in Classical Chinese Literature* (Cambridge: Harvard University Press, 1986).

27. Gian Biagio Conte, *The Rhetoric of Imitation: Genre of Poetic Memory in Virgil and Other Latin Poets,* ed. Charles Segal (Ithaca: Cornell University Press, 1986), p. 23. Also relevant is Thomas M. Greene's *The Light in Troy: Imitation and Discovery in Renaissance Poetry* (New Haven: Yale University Press, 1982), where he distinguishes reproductive (sacramental), eclectic (exploitative), heuristic, and dialectic imitations (pp. 38–45).

28. Conte, *Rhetoric of Imitation,* p. 52; Harry Caplan, *Of Eloquence: Studies in Ancient and Medieval Rhetoric,* ed. Anne King and Helen North (Ithaca: Cornell University Press, 1970), pp. 196–246.

29. James R. Hightower, "Allusion in the Poetry of T'ao Ch'ien," *Harvard Journal of Asiatic Studies* 31 (1971): 15.

30. Conte, *Rhetoric of Imitation,* pp. 51, 69.

31. Burton Watson, *Su Tung-p'o* (New York: Columbia University Press, 1965), p. 92.

32. For translation of these poems see David Hawkes, *Ch'u Tz'u: The Songs of the South* (Oxford: Clarendon, 1959), pp. 21–34, 59–80.

33. Ovid, *Metamorphosis,* 11.418; Brooks Otis, *Ovid as an Epic Poet* (Cambridge: Cambridge University Press, 1966), pp. 231–277.

34. Lois Fusek, "The 'Kao-t'ang Fu,' " *Monumenta Serica* 30 (1972–1973): 412–423.

35. For a translation see James R. Hightower, *The Poetry of T'ao Ch'ien* (Oxford: Clarendon, 1970), pp. 254–258.

36. No. 45 is by Kim Inhu (1510–1560); nos. 64 and 77 are by Song Sun (1493–1583); and nos. 44 and 70 are anonymous folk songs current in his day.

37. *Mencius,* 6A.20 (D. C. Lau, *Mencius* [Harmondsworth, Middlesex: Penguin, 1970], p. 170); 4A.2 (Lau, pp. 118–119); *Great Learning,* 10 (Wing-tsit Chan, *A Source Book in Chinese Philosophy* [Princeton: Princeton University Press, 1963], p. 92).

38. The black zither is said to have been invented by Wang Sanak of Koguryŏ; Wang changed the seven-stringed zither of Chin into a six-stringed instrument.

39. *Nogye chip* (in *Yijo myŏnghyŏn chip,* 3 [Seoul: Taedong munhwa yŏnguwŏn, 1973]), 2.29b–30a, 37a.

40. Ibid., 2.30a.

41. Ibid.

42. *Nogye chip,* 2.30b, 37a.

43. Ibid., 1.1a–3b.

44. Ibid., 2.34a, 37a.

45. Ibid., 3.27a–b. One theory proposes 1617 as the date of composition. The full title reads "In the Fall of the Year 1621, I Bathed with Chŏng Hangang in Pepper Well in Ulsan."

46. See Yi Sangbaek, *Hanguk sa* (Seoul: Ŭryu, 1962), 3:606–680; Yi Hyŏngsŏk, *Imjin chŏllan sa,* 3 vols. (Seoul: Ch'ungmuhoe, 1975).

47. Arthur Waley, *The Analects of Confucius* (London: Allen & Unwin, 1949), p. 117.

48. Ibid., p. 182.

49. For his biography see Burton Watson, *Records of the Grand Historian of China*, 2 vols. (New York: Columbia University Press, 1961), 1:508–516.

50. Arthur Waley, *The Book of Songs* (London: Allen & Unwin, 1954), p. 213.

51. Ben Jonson, "To Penshurst," lines 32–33; Thomas Carew, "To Sexham," lines 27–28.

52. Birch, *Anthology of Chinese Literature*, p. 210.

53. Waley, *Analects*, p. 88.

54. Ibid., p. 126.

55. Attributed to Shun. See James J. Y. Liu, *Chinese Theories of Literature* (Chicago: University of Chicago Press, 1975), p. 69.

56. Here Yun Sŏndo repeats *kilgo, mŏlgo, mank'o, hago,* and *ulgo.* Semantically, *hago* repeats the meaning of *mank'o* (endless), in effect repeating "endless" four times. My fourth line, "And my heart is heavy," tries to capture the poet's longing for his parents from his place of exile in the northeast. The last two lines literally go: "Somewhere, a wild goose / flies by crying crying."

57. Waley, *Analects*, p. 199.

58. Yi Usŏng proposes that the first author and singer of fisherman's songs might be Kong Pu, grandson of Kong Sŏ, who immigrated to Korea from China in the late fourteenth century. See "Koryŏ-mal Yijo-ch'o ŭi ŏbuga" (The fisherman's songs at the end of Koryŏ and beginning of Yi), *Sŏngdae nonmunjip* 9 (1964): 5–27, esp. 19–21.

59. Kim (d. 1348) served as Minister of the Left during the reign of the twenty-ninth king of Koryŏ. See *Koryŏ sa* (Seoul: Tongbanhak yŏnsugo ed., 1955), 104.31a–b.

60. He passed the examination in 1540 and became the Fourth Inspector.

61. Yi passed the examination in 1498 and held such posts as the Third Minister of Punishments, Second Minister of Personnel, and Governor of Kyŏngsang province. He was honest and stern and upon retirement built himself a hall by the Pun River in Yean. The waters crashing against the rocks were so powerful and loud that he named the place "Deaf Rocks" and adopted the term as his pen name. Yi Hwang studied under him, and Hwang Chullyang was Yi Hyŏngbo's best companion in his noble pursuit. For his "accounts of conduct" written by Yi Hwang see *Nongam sŏnsaeng munjip* (in *Yijo myŏnghyŏn chip,* 3), 4.1a–10b.

62. For their texts see *Nongam sŏnsaeng munjip,* 3.15a–16b.

63. *T'oegye chip* (Taedong munhwa yŏnguwŏn ed., 1958), 9.3a ff.

CHŎNG CH'ŎL

Kasa

1. Yŏnch'u Gate, the south gate of the palace in Seoul.

2. "Kyŏnghoe South Gate" in the original, probably the south gate to the Kyŏnghoe Tower, the site of royal banquets.

3. Token of delegated authority issued as a credential.

4. P'yŏnggu Station, forty-five *ri* east of Seoul. A *ri* is about one-third of a mile.

5. Seventy *ri* east of Yangju.

6. Sŏm River, the upper tributary of the Han, fifty *ri* southwest of Wŏnju.

7. Twenty-five *ri* east of Wŏnju.

8. Soyang River, six *ri* east of Ch'unch'ŏn.

9. Pukkwan Arbor, north of Ch'ŏrwŏn.

10. Kung Ye (r. 901–918) raised a rebellion against Silla and named his state T'aebong. He occupied the area of modern Ch'ŏrwŏn. See *Samguk sagi,* Yi Pyŏngdo ed. (Seoul: Ŭryu, 1977), 50.451–454.

11. A good administrator under Emperor Wu (140–86 B.C.) who died in 12 B.C. He was governor of Huai-yang (which is also the name of a town in Kangwŏn province). See *Shih chi,* 120.3105–3111; Burton Watson, *Records of the Grand Historian of China,* 2 vols. (New York: Columbia University Press, 1961), 2:343–352.

12. A valley northeast of the Changan monastery.

13. The name of a canyon from the top of the P'yohun monastery to the bottom of Magayŏn.

14. North of the P'yohun monastery, a stone terrace so steep no mortal can climb it. Only two black cranes have their nest on its summit.

15. An allusion to Su Shih, "The Red Cliff, 2." See Burton Watson, *Su Tung-p'o* (New York: Columbia University Press, 1965), p. 92: "It [a lone crane] wore a black robe and a coat of white silk."

16. Ch'ien-t'ang or Ming-sheng Lake. Lin Pu (967–1028) lived on a hill near the lake and amused himself by growing plum trees and keeping cranes.

17. North of the P'yohun monastery. A peak in front of the monastery is called Chinhol (True Rest) Terrace.

18. In Kiangsi. Li Po wrote a poem titled "Viewing the Waterfall at Mount Lu"; see Burton Watson, *The Columbia Book of Chinese Poetry: From Early Times to the Thirteenth Century* (New York: Columbia University Press, 1984), p. 209.

19. Manggo Terrace, east peak of the Diamond Mountains.

20. Hyŏlmang Peak, one of the highest peaks in the Diamond Mountains.

21. Kaesim Terrace, above the True Light Temple.

22. Chunghyang Castle, rugged peaks southeast of Yŏngnang.

23. The highest peak in the Diamond Mountains.

24. Both are in Shantung and mentioned, for example, in the *Book of Songs* (300), *Mencius* (2A.2 and 7A.24), and *Analects* (3.6).

25. Ssu-ma Ch'ien (145–90? B.C.) compared Confucius to a lofty mountain: "The great mountain, I look up to it; the great road, I travel it. Although I cannot reach it, my heart goes out toward it. When I read the works of Confucius, I try to imagine what sort of person he was." See Burton Watson, *Ssu-ma Ch'ien: Grand Historian of China* (New York: Columbia University Press, 1958), p. 173.

26. Wŏnt'ong Grotto, ravine north of the P'yohun monastery.

27. Rock in the shape of a lion, north of Yongsu. Fiery Dragon Pool is the deepest gorge in Myriad Falls Grotto.

28. An image of Maitreya was carved on a cliff three *ri* east of Magayŏn.

29. A hill called Anmun between Magayŏn and the Yujŏm monastery.

30. Pulchŏng Terrace, some sixty *ri* west of Kosŏng.

31. Mountain Glare Tower, the gate of the Yujŏm monastery, some sixty *ri* from Kosŏng.

32. Kŭmnan cave, twelve *ri* east of T'ongch'ŏn.

33. Eighteen *ri* north of T'ongch'ŏn. Dozens of hexagonal stone pillars soar from the sea forming a kind of pavilion, one of the Eight Scenes of Kwandong. The four knights of Silla are said to have visited the place, hence its name "Four Fairies Peak."

34. Artisan Ch'ui, a master craftsman of ancient China mentioned in the *Chuang Tzu*, 19: "Artisan Ch'ui could draw as true as a compass or a T square because his fingers changed with things and he didn't let his mind get in the way." See Burton Watson, *The Complete Works of Chuang Tzu* (New York: Columbia University Press, 1968), p. 206.

35. The four knights of Silla are said not to have returned after three days. The "six red letters" refer to a stone niche on a small peak to the south of Three Days Cove (Samilp'o); on the north precipice of the peak were written in red ink six Chinese logographs meaning, "We are going toward the south."

36. Eleven *ri* south.

37. Fifty-five *ri* south of Kansŏng.

38. Several *ri* east of Ch'ŏnggan Station, forty *ri* south of Kansŏng. Stone pillars rise from the sea and form a terrace with steps—one of the Eight Scenes of Kwandong.

39. Naksan monastery is fifteen *ri* northeast of Yangyang and a cave to the west is called Ŭisang Terrace. The monastery was built by the Great Master Ŭisang (625–702).

40. Mount Hyŏn, north Yangyang.

41. Fifteen *ri* northeast of Kangnŭng; one of the Eight Scenes of Kwandong.

42. Kangmun Bridge, at the eastern entrance to the lake.

43. A famous *kisaeng* of Kangnŭng who left one *sijo* poem. In *Tongin sihwa,* 2.64, Sŏ Kŏjŏng (1420–1489) says that she lived at the end of the fourteenth century. See Chang Hongjae ed. (Seoul: Hagusa, 1980), pp. 233–235.

44. Located 150 *ri* south of Samch'ŏk. It makes forty-seven turns from its source to Samch'ŏk—hence "Fifty River." The Pearl House is a guest house in Samch'ŏk; the West Bamboo (Chuksŏ) Tower nestles on a cliff west of the Pearl Harbor overlooking the Fifty River. One of the Eight Scenes of Kwandong.

45. A mountain range, called T'aebaek, that constitutes the backbone of the Korean peninsula.

46. Scorpii according to Joseph Needham, *Science and Civilization in China,* vol. 3 (Cambridge: Cambridge University Press, 1959), table 24.

47. Forty *ri* north of P'yŏnghae; one of the Eight Scenes of Kwandong.

48. In the original, "Flowing Mist" or "Streaming Cloud."

49. The most famous of the Mao Shan texts of Taoism. The poet is reminded of Su Shih's rhymeprose, "The Red Cliff, 2."

50. The Moon Palace is literally Kwanghan Kung (Great Cold Palace).

51. Two rivers that flow into Lake Tungt'ing in Hunan, rich in mythology and scenic beauty.

52. The Renowned Doctor was a famous physician (in the original P'ien Ch'üeh) during the Spring and Autumn period; *Shih chi,* 105.2785–2820.

53. Where the Taoist deities reside.

54. The lady of Witches' Mountain who appeared in Kiang Hsiang's (r. 298–265 B.C.) dream and said to him, "I live on the southern side of the Witches' Mountain, in the rocky crags of Kao-ch'iu. At dawn I am the Morning Cloud, and at dusk, the Driving Rain." See Lois Fusek, "The 'Kao-t'ang Fu,' " *Monumenta Serica* 30 (1972–1973): 413.

55. The summit of Mount Mudŭng in Kwangju.

56. The southeast gate of Ch'ang-an. When the dynasty changed, Shao P'ing, marquis of Tung-ling under the Ch'in, had to live by raising melons. His melons were called Blue Gate or Tung-ling melons. See Watson, *Records,* 1:130.

57. For T'ao Ch'ien's literary and political utopia see James R. Hightower, *The Poetry of T'ao Ch'ien* (Oxford: Clarendon, 1970), pp. 254–258.

58. The ancient worthy refers to a hermit said to have lived before the time of Fu Hsi, a Chinese culture hero.

59. Chou (1017–1073) is the author of the *Diagram of the Supreme Ultimate Explained,* which elucidates the origins of "Heavenly Principles."

60. T'ai-i (Great One or Unique) is the supreme sky god in Chinese mythology who resides in the palace at the Center of Heaven, marked by the polestar. See Needham, *Science and Civilization in China,* 3:260.

61. On Mount West Lake in Hu-chou.

62. "In the autumn of the year *jen-hsü,* the seventh month, when the moon had just passed its prime, a friend and I went out in a small boat to amuse ourselves at the foot of the Red Cliff"; see Watson, *Su Tung-p'o,* p. 87.

63. When Emperor Yao wished to make the recluse Hsü Yu his successor, the latter went into hiding. At the emperor's second offer, Hsü Yu went to the Ying River to cleanse his ears.

64. The name of a *tz'u* (lyric) tune.

Sijo

1. The following sixteen poems, written when the poet was governor of Kangwŏn province (1580), are inspired by Ch'en Ku-liang (Ch'en Hsiang, 1017–1080), *Hsien-chü ch'üan-yü-wen,* in the *Hsiao-hsüeh chi-chu (SPPY),* 5.7a–b. See Yi Pyŏngju, ed., *Songgang Kosan munhak non* [Studies in the Poetry of Chŏng Ch'ŏl and Yun Sondo] (Seoul: Iu ch'ulp'ansa, 1979), pp. 49–77.

2. Corresponds to 3 to 5 A.M.

3. Literally, Pongnae Mountain, one of the mountains in the fairy islands in the eastern sea where immortals dwell; here and elsewhere (poem 28) used for the royal palace. In some poems Pongnae Mountain refers to South Mountain, which lies south of Seoul.

4. Liu Ling (died after 265), the author of "Hymn to the Virtue of Wine" and one of the Seven Worthies of the Bamboo Grove.

5. Kyeham is the poet's polite name.

6. In poems 24–27 the poet holds an imaginary dialogue with wine ("your" in line 1).

7. The name of a Chinese commandery in the northeast later absorbed by Koguryŏ in the early fourth century.

8. Shin Ŭngsi (1532–1585), governor of Chŏlla province and Censor-General; the South Gate is the entrance to the audience hall.

9. The star Canopus.

10. Sinwŏn is in Koyang, Kyŏnggi.

11. Chia Yi (201–169 B.C.), tutor to the king of Ch'ang-sha in the south.

12. The sacred mountain—center of the world and supporter of the skies. This poem has more metric segments than the regular *sijo*.

13. Sŏng Hon (1535–1598), the poet's teacher. As Sixth State Counselor he assisted the crown prince during the Japanese invasion; he opposed the metaphysical theories of Yi I.

14. Office of Special Counselors; its members drafted state papers and conducted research on adminstrative and legal precedents.

15. Ko Kyŏngmyŏng (d. 1592), leader of six thousand troops at Kŭmsan, died in battle against the Japanese invaders.

16. King Myŏngjong granted Song Sun (1493–1582), counselor in the Office of Special Counselors (also known as Jade Hall), the true author of this poem, a spray of chrysanthemums, a symbol of unchanging ties between sovereign and subject.

17. Kwŏn P'il (1568–1638), a pupil of Chŏng Ch'ŏl, cites a heptasyllabic quatrain in Chinese of this folk song current in the sixteenth century. See his *Sŏkchu chip* (1674 ed.), 7.27a; also in *Songgang chŏnjip*, p. 440.

18. The final three poems, which are not in the Sŏngju edition, are contained in the Hwangju edition.

PAK ILLO

Kasa

1. The uncle of the last monarch of the Shang dynasty, who is said to have fled to Korea in 1122 B.C. when the Shang was deposed by the Chou and to have built a capital at P'yŏngyang. Traditionally his dynasty lasted until 194 B.C.

2. *Sun Tzu*, 7.28b–34a; see Samuel B. Griffith, *Sun Tzu: The Art of War* (Oxford: Clarendon, 1963), p. 110: "Do not press an enemy at bay."

3. Refers to Sŏng Yunmun (fl. 1591–1607), Regional Commander of the Left Bank. The original text compares him to Chu-ko Liang (181–234), reputed to be the greatest Chinese strategist of all time.

4. Wisdom, sincerity, benevolence, courage, and strictness.

5. Refers to the Ming mediator between Korea and Japan, Shen Wei-ching. On eloquence see *Book of Songs*, 260.3; Bernhard Karlgren, *The Book of Odes* (Stockholm: Museum of Far Eastern Antiquities, 1950), pp. 228–229.

6. Su Shih, "The Red Cliff, 1" (Burton Watson, *Su T'ung-p'o* [New York:

Columbia University Press, 1965], p. 89): "The stems and sterns of his [Ts'ao Ts'ao; 155–200] ships touched for a thousand miles, and his flags and pennants blocked out the sky."

7. A pejorative reference to Katō Kiyomasa (1562–1611).

8. *Mencius,* 2B.1; see D. C. Lau, *Mencius* (Harmondsworth, Middlesex: Penguin, 1970), p. 85: "Heaven's favorable weather is less important than Earth's advantageous terrain, and Earth's advantageous terrain is less important than human unity."

9. *Han-shih wai-chuan,* 5.12; J. R. Hightower, *Han Shih Wai Chuan: Han Ying's Illustrations of the Didactic Application of the Classic of Songs* (Cambridge: Harvard University Press, 1952), pp. 171–172: "In the time of great peace there are no sudden winds or violent rains or waves and inundations on the sea."

10. Hsi-liu Ying in the southwest of Hsien-yang in Shensi, where troops under Chou Ya-fu (d. 143 B.C.) once made their encampment. See H. H. Dubs, *The History of the Former Han Dynasty* (Baltimore: Waverly Press, 1938), 1:269–299, 326, and n. 8.6: "In B.C. 174 he was appointed to a command against the Hsiung-nu, who were then invading the empire, and when the Emperor Wen presented himself at his stronghold, his Majesty was unable to gain admittance until Chou himself had given orders for the gate to be opened."

11. While T'ang T'ai-tsung, still as the Prince of Ch'in, was subjugating the four quarters, there was a piece of music named "Ch'in-wang p'o-chen-yüeh" in circulation. The earliest record of its performance dates from 627. In 633 T'ai-tsung ordered the choreographic diagram "P'o-chen-wu t'u" to be drawn up and instructed Lü Ts'ai to teach one hundred and twenty musicians to perform the dance according to the diagram. Later this dance was called the Dance of the Seven Virtues. The first reference to the seven virtues occurs in the *Tso Commentary,* Duke Hsüan 12 (James Legge, *The Chinese Classics* [Hong Kong: University of Hong Kong Press, 1960], 5:320). They are as follows: repressing cruelty; calling in the weapons of war; preserving the great appointment; firmly establishing one's merit; giving repose to the people; harmonizing all the state; and enlarging the general wealth.

12. Mount Hua is the western sacred mountain in Kiangsu.

13. In Sinkiang.

14. A Chinese culture hero; inventor of writing, fishing, and trapping.

15. *Mencius,* 2B.4; see Lau, *Mencius,* p. 88: "In the years of famine close on a thousand of your people suffered, the old and the young being abandoned in the gutter, the able-bodied scattered in all directions."

16. James Legge, *The Li Ki* (Oxford: Clarendon, 1885), p. 131: "The ancients had a saying, that a fox, when dying, adjusts its head in the direction of the mound [where it was whelped]; manifesting thereby [how it shares in the feeling of] humanity."

17. *Book of Songs,* 258.3; Karlgren, *Book of Odes,* pp. 223 f.: "The drought is excessive, it cannot be removed; it is fearsome, it is terrible, like lightning, like thunder; of the crowd of people that remained of the Chou, there is not an undamaged body left."

18. The dynasties of Hsia, Shang (Yin), and Chou.

19. A song that eulogized the blessing of peace under Emperor Yao (*Ku-shih yüan* [*SPPY*], 1.1a), translated by Burton Watson, *The Columbia Book of Chinese Poetry: From Early Times to the Thirteenth Century,* (New York: Columbia University Press, 1984)p. 70.

20. The year 1605.

21. The Yellow Emperor was thought to be the inventor of wheeled vehicles, ships, armor, and pottery, among other things.

22. *Book of Songs,* 205.2; see Arthur Waley, *The Book of Songs* (London: Allen & Unwin, 1954), p. 320.

23. *Shih chi,* 6.247.

24. Here the poet argues that descendants of those "boys and maidens" settled on Japanese islands and became ancestors of the Japanese people.

25. Or Hsü Fu, who persuaded the First Emperor of Ch'in to send out an expedition of several thousand young men and women to search for the Isles of the Blest, thought to be inhabited by immortals. See, for example, Po Chü-i's poem "Magic" in Arthur Waley, *A Hundred and Seventy Chinese Poems* (New York: Knopf, 1919), pp. 195–196.

26. Chang (c. 258–319) took office with Prince Ching of Ch'i but resigned because "he could not do without the salad and bream of the Sung River in Kiangsu"; *Chin Shu* (Peking: Chung-hua shu-chü, 1974), 92.2384.

27. This phrase comes from a poem by Tai Shih-ping, "Shih-ping shih-chi" (*SPTK hsü-pien* I), 7.5b. The three dukes were originally the three ministers of state in Chou, the grand tutor, the grand assistant, and the grand guardian, but in Korea the term "three dukes" refers to the chief, second, and third state counselors.

28. Su Shih, "The Red Cliff, I" (Watson, *Su Tung-p'o,* p. 90): "Among the litter of cups and bowls, we lay down in a heap in the bottom of the boat, unaware that the east was already growing light."

29. *Analects,* 2.1; see Arthur Waley, *The Analects of Confucius* (London: Allen & Unwin, 1949), p. 88: "The Master said, He who rules by moral force

(te) is like the polestar, which remains in its place while all the lesser stars do homage to it."

30. An allusion to the story of Ssu-ma I (178–251), who was frightened by the dead Chu-ko Liang (181–234): "In this month [Chu-ko] Liang died, with the army. The *chiang-shih* Yang I put the army in order and marched off; the population rushed off to Ssu-ma I and informed him, and I pursued them. Chiang Wei ordered [Yang] I to turn the banners and beat the drums, as if intending to meet I. I thereupon departed, with his troops in battle formation. Entering [Yeh-] ku he announced the death of [Chu-ko Liang]. The people made it a saying, 'Dead Chu-ko has put live Chung-ta to flight!' " See Achilles Fang, *The Chronicles of the Three Kingdoms* (Cambridge: Harvard University Press, 1952), pp. 435–436.

31. An allusion to the story of how Sun Pin of Ch'i defeated the Wei army of P'ang Chüan (*Shih chi,* 65.2162).

32. An allusion to the story of Chu-ko Liang, the chief minister of Liu Pei of the Shu kingdom, capturing and releasing Meng Hao seven times. *San-kuo chih,* 35, *Shu shu,* 5.911–937, esp. 921.

33. See note 9 above.

34. *Hou Ch'u-shih piao* of Chu-ko Liang. See Lin Yin, ed., *Liang-Han San-kuo wen-hui* (Taipei: Taiwan shu-tien, 1960), p. 1755.

35. *Book of Songs,* 260.4 (Karlgren, *Book of Odes,* p. 229): "Morning and evening he [Chung Shan-fu] does not slacken in the service of the One Man."

36. The I River was the abode of Ch'eng I (1033–1108), generally referred to as "the master of the I River." The Wei is in Shensi, where T'ai-kung Wang spent his time fishing.

37. Mount Fu-ch'un is where Yen Kuang, a contemporary of Emperor Kuang-wu, retired. Mount Chi is in Honan, where Ch'ao-fu and Hsü Yu retired.

38. In Fukien, where Chu Hsi lived.

39. P'an Valley in Honan, twenty *li* north of Chi-yüan *hsien.*

40. Fan Chung-yen (989–1052), *Yo-yang-lou chi,* in *Fan Wen-cheng-kung chi (SPTK),* 7.3b. For Fan see James T. C. Liu, "An Early Sung Reformer: Fan Chung-yen," in *Chinese Thought and Institutions,* ed. John K. Fairbank (Chicago: University of Chicago Press, 1957), pp. 105–131.

41. The six types of domestic animals: horses, cattle, sheep, goats, fowl, and dogs.

42. *Analects,* 11.24 (Waley, *Analects,* p. 160): "Tseng Hsi said, At the end of spring, When the making of the Spring Clothes have been completed, to go

with five times six newly-capped youths and six times seven uncapped boys, perform the lustration in the river I, take the air at the Rain Dance altars, and then going home singing."

43. The first trip took place in the seventh month, and the second trip in the tenth month, of 1082.

44. The Fashioner of Creatures or Mutations, or the old man who fashions creatures, is a shaper and molder of matter—a metaphysical principle responsible for the multiplicity and particularity of the phenomenal world. See Edward H. Schafer, "The Idea of Created Nature in T'ang Literature," *Philosophy East and West* 15 (1965): 153–160.

45. Young crows, paragons of filial piety, are said to disgorge food in order to feed their parents.

46. Legge, *Li Ki,* p. 67: "In the evening, to adjust to everything [for their repose], and to inquire [about their health] in the morning."

47. One of the twenty-four examples of filial piety. "At seventy, he was still accustomed to divert his aged parents by dressing himself up and cutting capers before them." See *Kao-shih chuan* (Lives of High-Minded Gentlemen), 1.7a.

48. *Analects,* 6.11 (Waley, *Analects,* pp. 117–118): "Incomparable indeed was Hui! A handful of rice to eat, a gourdful of water to drink, living in a mean street."

49. *Book of Songs,* 250 (Karlgren, *Book of Odes,* pp. 206–207): "Staunch was Prince Liu . . . he tied up provisions in bags, in sacks."

50. The phrase occurs in Han Yü's poem "To Lu T'ang," for which see *Ch'ang-li hsien-sheng chi (SPPY),* 5.3a–b. For the German translation of the poem see Erwin von Sach, *Han Yüs Poetische Werke* (Cambridge: Harvard University Press, 1952), p. 123.

51. "The Return" of T'ao Ch'ien (James R. Hightower, *The Poetry of T'ao ch'ien* [Oxford: Clarendon, 1970], p. 269): "The farmers tell me that now spring is here / There will be work to do in the west fields."

52. I Yin, minister under Ch'eng T'ang (r. 1766–1754 B.C.); see *Mencius,* 5A.7 (Lau, *Mencius,* p. 146).

53. Ch'en Sheng (or She); see Burton Watson, *Records of the Grand Historian of China,* 2 vols. (New York: Columbia University Press, 1961), 1:19–33: "When Ch'en She was young, he was working one day in the fields with the other hired men. Suddenly he stopped his plowing and went and stood on a hillock, wearing a look of profound discontent. After a long while he announced, 'If I become rich and famous, I will not forget the rest of you.' The

other farm hands laughed and answered, 'You are nothing but a hired laborer. How could you ever become rich and famous?' Ch'en She gave a great sigh, 'Oh, well,' he said, 'how could you little sparrows be expected to understand the ambitions of a swan?' "

54. *Book of Songs,* 55.1 (Waley, *Book of Songs,* p. 47): "Look at that little bay of the Ch'i, / Its kitefoot so delicately waving."

55. *Analects,* 14.11 (Waley, *Analects,* p. 182): "To be poor and not resent it is far harder than to be rich, yet not presumptuous."

56. *Book of Songs,* 194.6 (Karlgren, *Book of Odes,* p. 141).

57. In Fukien, thirty *li* south of Ch'ung-an *hsien.*

58. Su Shih, "The Red Cliff, 1" (Watson, *Su Tung-p'o,* p. 90): "Moreover, everything in this world has its owner; and if a thing doesn't belong to us, we don't dare take a hair of it. Only the clear breeze over the river, or the bright moon between the hills, which our ears hear as music, our eyes see beauty in— these we may take without prohibition, these we may make free with and they will never be used up."

59. Disciples of Confucius.

60. *Mencius,* 5B.8 (Lau, *Mencius,* p. 158). "He" refers to Yi Ŏnjŏk.

61. A retreat of Ssu-ma Kuang (1019–1086) in Honan, south of Loyang. He was a native of Shensi and a leading opponent of Wang An-shih (1021–1086).

62. T'oegye is the pen name of Yi Hwang (1501–1571), perhaps the most famous Neo-Confucian philosopher of the Chosŏn dynasty.

63. See *Kung-tzu chia-yü (SPPY),* 4.4a.

64. Li Kung-lin (1070–1106) of Sung lived on Mount Lung-mien and excelled in verse and painting.

65. *Book of Songs,* 293.3 (Karlgren, *Book of Odes,* p. 191): "The hawk flies and reaches heaven; the fish leaps in the deep."

66. Chou Tun-i (1017–1073), the pioneer of Neo-Confucianism in Sung China.

67. In Kiangsi; also called Nan-chang Shan, celebrated in the poems of Li Po and Su Shih.

68. Allusion to "The Fisherman," for which see David Hawkes, trans., *Ch'u Tz'u: The Songs of the South* (Oxford: Clarendon, 1959), pp. 90–91, esp. 91.

69. Lu Chi's "Rhymeprose on Literature," in Cyril Birch, ed., *Anthology of Chinese Literature: From Early Times to the Fourteenth Century* (New York: Grove Press, 1965), p. 210: "Let it [meaning], then, be contained like jade in rocks, that a mountain loom in radiance, / Or cast it like a pearl in water that a whole river gleam with splendor."

70. Li Po, "Climbing Phoenix Terrace at Chin-ling"; Wu-chi Liu and Irving Y. Lo, eds., *Sunflower Splendor* (Garden City: Doubleday, 1975), p. 113.

71. In Chekiang.

72. Fan Chung-yen (989–1052), author of the *Yo-yang-lou chi.*

73. Refers to a tradition that Shun longed for Yao for three years after his death and saw his image on the walls whenever he sat and in the soup whenever he ate.

74. *Book of Songs,* 4.1; 125.1–5; 222.3–5 (Karlgren, *Book of Odes,* pp. 4, 116–117, 176).

75. Hou Chi or Lord Millet, inventor of agriculture, ancestor of the Chou people; *Book of Songs,* 245.1 (Waley, *Book of Songs,* p. 241). Chieh was a wise minister under Shun.

76. Such men as Shao Yung (1011–1077), Ssu-ma Kuang (1019–1086), Ch'eng I (I-ch'uan, 1033–1107), and Chang Tsai (Heng-ch'u, 1020–1077).

77. Tzu-yang Shan is the place where Chu Sung (1097–1143), father of Chu Hsi, lived.

78. *Great Learning,* 1; see Wing-tsit Chan, *A Source Book in Chinese Philosophy* (Princeton: Princeton University Press, 1963), p. 86: "The ancients who wished to bring order to their states would first regulate their families. Those who wished to regulate their families would first cultivate their personal lives. Those who wished to cultivate their personal lives would first rectify their minds. Those who wished to rectify their minds would first make their wills sincere. Those who wished to make their wills sincere would first extend their knowledge. The extension of knowledge consists in the investigation of things."

79. *Analects,* 15.6 (Waley, *Analects,* p. 194): "Be loyal and true to your every word, serious and careful in all you do."

80. The eastern sacred mountain in China.

81. *Great Learning,* 1 (Chan, *Source Book,* p. 86): "The way of learning to be great consists in manifesting the clear character, loving the people, and abiding in the highest good."

82. *Doctrine of the Mean,* 20 (Chan, *Source Book,* p. 105): "There are nine standards by which to administer the empire, its states, and the families. There are: cultivating the personal life, honoring the worthy, being affectionate to relatives, being respectful toward the great minister, identifying oneself with the welfare of the whole body of officers, treating the common people as one's own children, attracting the various artisans, showing tenderness to strangers from far countries, and extending kindly and awesome influence on the feudal lords." For the Eight Virtues, see *sijo,* note 32.

83. *Great Learning,* 9.2 (Legge, *Chinese Classics,* 1.234): "Act as if you were watching over an infant. If a mother is really anxious about it, though she may not hit exactly the wants of her infant, she will not be far from doing so."

84. *Chuang Tzu,* 26; see Burton Watson, *The Complete Works of Chuang Tzu* (New York: Columbia University Press, 1968), p. 295: "Chuang Chou's family was very poor and so he went to borrow some grain from the marquis of Chien-ho. The marquis said, 'Why, of course. I'll soon be getting the tribute money from my fief, and when I do, I'll be glad to lend you three hundred pieces of gold. Will that be all right?'

"Chuang Chou flushed with anger and said, 'As I was coming here yesterday, I heard someone calling me on the road. I turned around and saw that there was a perch in the carriage rut. I said to him, "Come, perch—what are you doing here?" He replied, "I am a Wave Official of the Eastern Sea. Couldn't you give me a dipperful of water so I can stay alive?" I said to him, "Why, of course. I'm just about to start south to visit the kings of Wu and Yüeh. I'll change the course of the West River and send it in your direction. Will that be all right?" The perch flushed with anger and said, "I've lost my element! I have nowhere to go! If you can get me a dipper of water, I'll be able to stay alive. But if you give me an answer like that, then you'd best look for me in the dried fish store!" ' "

85. *Book of Songs,* 220.1 (Karlgren, *Book of Odes,* p. 171): "The bows with their arrows are stringed."

86. Allusion to Tu Fu's poem " A Recruiting Officer at Shih-hao" in Liu and Lo, *Sunflower Splendor,* pp. 130–131.

87. In the original: "Are we not living in the time of Wu-huai? / Are we not living in the time of Ko-t'ien?" Both Wu-huai and Ko-t'ien are legendary rulers. My translation here and in "Song of the Reedy Stream" reads: ". . . enjoy golden days of peace." For a reference to them in T'ao Ch'ien's "Biography of the Gentleman of the Five Willows," see A. R. Davis, *T'ao Yüan-ming (A.D. 365–427): His Works and Their Meaning* (Cambridge: Cambridge University Press), 1:208.

88. *Analects,* 12.13 (Waley, *Analects,* p. 167): "The Master said, I could try a civil suit as well as anyone. But better still to bring it about that there were no civil suits."

89. Refers to a tradition that when the legendary Emperor Shun went to Mount Li he was given a field, and when he went to Lei Stream he was given a good place for fishing (*Shih chi,* 1.33–34).

90. As prefect of Pa-tung subprefecture, K'ou Chun (961–1023) planted a

pair of cedar trees, following the example of the sweet pear trees planted in honor of the good administration of the Duke of Shao; *Book of Songs,* 16 (Waley, *Book of Songs,* p. 135).

91. The year 1636.

92. Guardian symbols of the four corners according to the ancient Chinese pseudoscience.

93. Refers to T'ao Ch'ien, known as "the gentleman of the five willows."

94. Two recluses of the state of Ch'u (*Analects,* 18.6).

95. *Mencius,* 2A.2. D. C. Lau translates it "flood-like *ch'i*" (*Mencius,* p. 77); Wing-tsit Chan offers "strong, moving power" (*Source Book,* p. 63).

96. *Mencius,* 4A.20 (Lau, *Mencius,* p. 126).

97. Perhaps a reference to T'ao Ch'ien, "Untitled Poems," 6: "If I fail to leave my sons a cent / I need not bother about a will" (Hightower, *Poetry of T'ao ch'ien,* p. 192). See also T'ao's "Testament" to his sons in Hightower, *Poetry of T'ao ch'ien,* p. 5.

Sijo

1. This poem is said to have been inspired by an anecdote connected with Lu Chi (late second to early third century) who at age six carried three oranges for his mother.

2. Wang Hsiang (185–269), a paragon of filial piety who at the end of the Han dynasty fled with his stepmother to her old home and looked after her for thirty years.

3. Meng Tsung (third century), official in the kingdom of Wu, who is known for filial devotion to his mother.

4. Master Tseng, a disciple of Confucius, another filial son.

5. A Chinese culture hero and the inventor of agriculture.

6. *Analects,* 11.24 (Waley, *Analects,* p. 160).

7. Chu Hsi (1130–1200), the Sung synthesizer of Neo-Confucianism.

8. *Analects,* 9.11 (Waley, *Analects,* p. 140): "The more I [Yen Hui] strain my gaze up toward it [goodness], the higher it soars. The deeper I bore down into it, the harder it becomes."

9. *Analects,* 16.4 (Waley, *Analects,* p. 205): "There are three sorts of friend that are profitable . . . friendship with the upright, with the true-to-death, and with those who have heard much."

10. Rules and regulations necessary for good government and individual moral conduct—an allusion to *Mencius,* 4A.1.

11. *Mencius,* 5A.7 (Lau, *Mencius,* p. 146): "I have never heard of anyone who can right others by bending himself."

12. Yen Kuang (37 B.C.–A.D. 43), a friend and adviser to Emperor Kuang-wu (r. 25–58), lived as a fisherman in modern Chekiang because he wished to refuse the latter's offer of a high post.

13. The original reads twelve *hoe*, which makes up one *wŏn*, reckoned as 4,560 years; hence five millennia.

14. *Analects*, 3.8 (Waley, *Analects*, p. 96): "The Master said, Shang [Tzu-hsia] it is who bears me up. At last I have someone with whom I can discuss the *Songs!*"

15. *Book of Songs*, 195 (Karlgren, *Book of Odes*, p. 143): "Tremble, be cautious, as if approaching a deep abyss, as if treading on thin ice!"

16. *Analects*, 14.35 (Waley, *Analects*, p. 189): "The Master said, the studies of men below are felt on high, and perhaps after all I am known."

17. *Shang shu*, 7.7b (Legge, *Chinese Classics*, 3.350): "In raising a mound of nine fathoms the work is unfinished for want of one basket of earth."

18. *Mencius*, 7A.24 (Lau, *Mencius*, p. 187): "When Confucius ascended the Eastern Mount, [he] felt that the Lu was small."

19. Allusion to *Mencius*, 4B.14.

20. The Lo and I are associated with Sung Neo-Confucianists Ch'eng I (1033–1107) and Ch'eng Hao (1032–1085) because they lived nearby.

21. Four whiteheads retired to Mount Shang in disapproval of the Ch'in tyranny—symbols of high standards of integrity.

22. *Mencius*, 4A.28 (Lau, *Mencius*, p. 127): "Shun did everything that was possible to serve his parents. . . . This is the supreme achievement of a dutiful son."

23. *Analects*, 2.5 (Waley, *Analects*, p. 89): "The Master said, while they are alive, serve them according to ritual. When they die, bury them according to ritual and sacrifice to them according to ritual."

24. In the original "Lord Millet and Chieh": the first was the ancestor of the Chou people who taught them the cultivation of the five grains; the second, Grand Instructor under Shun, helped Yü to control the floodwaters.

25. Allusion to line 105 of "Encountering Sorrow" by Ch'ü Yüan (Hawkes, *Ch'u Tz'u*, p. 29).

26. Allusion to *Book of Songs*, 164.7 (Waley, *Book of Songs*, p. 204).

27. The wife of Hsi Chi (fl. 626–589 B.C.) in the state of Chin was a paragon of wifely virtues.

28. The wife of Liang Hung of the Later Han (*Hou Han shu* [Peking: Chung-hua shu-chü, 1962], 113.2675–2678).

29. The poet's two younger brothers died before him.

30. When King Wu decided to chastise the wicked last king of the Shang.

31. Near Yŏngch'ŏn, Kyŏngsang province.

32. The Three Bonds (between ruler and minister, father and son, and husband and wife) plus the Five Relations comprised the Eight Virtues: filial piety, brotherly subordination, loyalty, sincerity, propriety, righteousness, modesty, and a sense of shame.

YUN SŎNDO

1. The south gate in Kyŏngwŏn. *Kosan yugo,* 1.16a.

2. Refers to "The Fisherman" in *Ch'u Tz'u: The Songs of the South* (David Hawkes, trans. [Oxford: Clarendon, 1959] pp. 90–91).

3. The poet is referring ironically to his mode of life. This poem is also cited as a refrain *(yŏŭm)* at the end of "The Angler's Calendar." See *Kosan yugo,* 6B.15a.

4. See Chŏng Ch'ŏl, note 62.

5. In the original, Mount Wŏlch'ul, five *ri* south of Yongam.

6. The office that aided the people in times of need by lending them rice and other grains in the spring against repayment in the autumn.

7. Po I, together with his brother Shu Ch'i, disapproved of the Chou conquest of their overlord the Shang king and retired to Shou-yang mountain; resolving "not to eat the corn of Chou," they died of starvation. *Shih chi,* 61.2121–2129; Cyril Birch, ed., *Anthology of Chinese Literature: From Early Times to the Fourteenth Century* (New York: Grove Press, 1965), pp. 103–105.

8. The underworld.

9. *Book of Songs,* 219.1 (Bernhard Karlgren, *The Book of Odes,* [Stockholm: Museum of Far Eastern Antiquities, 1950], p. 172): "The green flies go buzzing about, they settle on the fence; joyous and pleasant lord, do not believe slanderous words."

10. This poem was addressed to Kwŏn Hae, the poet's close friend, whose pen name was Pangŭm, "companion of the zither." *Kosan yugo,* 4.24a.

11. *Shang shu (SPTK),* 5.9b (James Legge, *The Chinese Classics* [Hong Kong: University of Hong Kong Press, 1960], 3.253): "Wood, by the use of the line, is made straight; and the sovereign who follows reproof becomes sage."

12. *Shang shu,* 5.10b (Legge, *Chinese Classics,* 3:260): "Do you teach me what should be my aims. Be to me as the yeast and the malt in making sweet spirit; as the salt and the prunes in making agreeable soup."

13. *Shang shu,* 8.7b (Legge, *Chinese Classics,* 3:403): "King Wen told and instructed you youngsters the principal officers and [lower] managers of

affairs to avoid the constant [use] of wine. In the various states the drinking [should be] only at the sacrifices, and by virtue they hold on to sobriety."

14. Another version of lines 7–8 reads: "In the deep and clear stream, / All kinds of fishes are leaping." See Sim Chaewan, *Kyobon yŏktae sijo chŏnsŏ* [Complete canon of sijo, collated] (Seoul: Sejong munhwasa, 1972), no. 2176, pp. 770–772.

15. This again refers to "The Fisherman" in *Ch'u Tz'u*.

16. Lines 4–5 refer to Wu Yüan, a native of Ch'u. Denounced by Fu Ch'ai of Wu, he committed suicide. Fu was angry and caused his body to be put into a leather sack and thrown into the Wu River; on the bank the people raised a shrine to his memory (*Shih chi,* 66.2180).

17. Lines 7–8 refer to Ch'ü Yüan (c. 343–278 B.C.), who drowned himself in the Milo (or Ch'u) River. *Shih chi,* 84.2481–2491; Burton Watson, *Records of the Grand Historian of China,* 2 vols. (New York: Columbia University Press, 1961), 1:499–508, esp. 507.

18. Refers to a tradition that when the Emperor Shun went to Mount Li he was given a field, and when he went to Lei Stream he was given a good place for fishing (*Shih chi,* 1.33–34).

19. In the original, Minister Sang: Sang Hung-yang (152–80 B.C.). It is not clear why Sang is brought in to serve as a duplicitous courtier here. For Sang see *Shih chi,* 30.1428–1442.

20. Lines 4–5 refer to Wei Ying-wu (b. 736), "West Creek at Ch'u-chou"; see Burton Watson, *The Columbia Book of Chinese Poetry: From Early Times to the Thirteenth Century* (New York: Columbia University Press, 1984), p. 278.

21. The Phoenix Tower is the palace. In East Asian mythology, the rabbit is pounding magic medicine in the moon.

22. In their struggles for power, Wang Tao (276–339) referred to Yü Liang (289–340) as being filthy as dust. The wind is a "west wind" probably because Yü Liang served as General Chastizing the West. "A strong wind started to raise the dust, and Wang [Tao], whisking it away with his fan, said 'Yü Liang's dust is contaminating me!' " See Richard B. Mather, trans., *A New Account of Tales of the World* (Minneapolis: University of Minnesota Press, 1976), p. 429.

23. The Hsiao and Hsiang and Tungt'ing Lake are in northeastern Hunan.

24. In 817, the T'ang general Li Su took Ts'ai-chou in Honan by surprise and captured Wu Yüan-chi (783–817). Appearing before the enemy stronghold on a snowy night he had the wildfowl flushed from the numerous ponds outside the walls so that their noise might drown the sound of the approaching

army (*Chiu T'ang shu* [Peking: Chung-hua shu-chü, 1975], 133.3680; *Hsin T'ang shu* [Peking: Chung-hua shu-chü, 1975], 154.4877).

25. The king of the Former Ch'in, Fu Chien (338–385), attacked the Eastern Chin and suffered a crushing defeat (383). The retreating army feared ambush in every tree and tuft of grass and was alarmed by the sound of the wind and the whoop of cranes (*Chin shu,* 114.2918).

26. The original refers to "fish with big mouths and delicate scales"; Su Shih, "The Red Cliff, 2" (Burton Watson, *Su Tung-p'o* [New York: Columbia University Press, 1965], p. 91).

27. Yen Kuang (37 B.C.–A.D. 43), a contemporary of Emperor Kuang-wu, retired to Mount Fu-ch'un and spent his time fishing because he wished to decline the latter's offer of a high post (*Hou Han shu,* 113.2763–2764).

28. Refers to T'ai Kung Wang or Lü Shang, a counselor to King Wen of Chou who found him fishing in the Wei River. He was the subject of poems by Li Po and Po Chü-i. *Shih chi,* 32.1477–1481.

SOURCES

Chŏng Ch'ŏl

The *Collected Works of Chŏng Ch'ŏl (Songgang sŏnsaeng munjip* or simply *Songgang chip)* was compiled and published by his descendant in 1894 in eleven chapters in seven volumes. It also includes a chronological biography *(yŏnbo)* compiled in 1674. The *Works* contains the complete canon of the poet's verse and prose in Chinese: penta- and heptasyllabic quatrains *(chüeh-chü)* and regulated verse *(lü-shih)*, heptasyllabic old-style poetry *(ku-shih)* and regulated couplets *(p'ai-lü)*, and rhymeprose; memorials, communications, sacrificial speeches, letters, and miscellany; as well as an account of conduct and accounts written by others, accounts of the posthumous epithet, an inscription on the avenue to the grave, an epitaph, and a brief prose biography.

There are altogether five editions of the *Pine River Anthology (Songgang kasa)*, which contains Chŏng's Korean poems. The Kwanbuk and Ŭisŏng editions are no longer extant. The Hwangju edition (or Yi Sŏn or Ilsa edition; 1690) was discovered in June 1936 by the late Pang Chonghyŏn (1905–1952; Ilsa is his pen name) in Seoul. This edition consists of twenty-six sheets altogether; unlike the Sŏngju edition, it is not divided into chapters. Each page has ten lines, twenty letters to a line. The book contains five *kasa* and fifty-one *sijo* poems; three appear only in this edition. The book bears a postscript by Yi Sŏn (1632–1692) dated the first month of 1690 at Kijang in South Kyŏngsang province. The fourth, the Sŏngju edition (1747), is the most complete edition of the anthology still extant. Compiled by Chŏng Kwanha, the poet's fifth-generation descendant, the book consists of forty-four sheets and is divided into two chapters. The first chapter consists of twenty-four sheets containing five *kasa;* the second chapter consists of eighteen sheets with seventy-nine *sijo* poems. Each page has eight lines, and every line has sixteen letters. This edition bears two postscripts, one (dated 1698) by Chŏng Chon (1659–1724) and one (dated 1747) by Chŏng Kwanha. The fifth is the Kwansŏ edition (P'yŏngyang, 1768). It is based on the Ŭisŏng edition and has no chapter divisions. The book, which consists of twenty-three sheets (ten lines to a sheet and twenty-two letters to a line), was discovered in July 1948 and is now preserved in the National Central Library in Seoul.

A curious feature of the Hwangju and Kwansŏ editions is that they also contain Chinese poems by other poets: a poem by Yun Iji (1589–1668) and another by Kim Sanghŏn (1570–1652); a heptasyllabic quatrain and a eulogy by Kwŏn P'il (1569–1612) are appended after "The Wanderings" in both editions. Also, the "Continued Hymn of Constancy" is followed by a heptasyllabic quatrain "On Hearing the *Songgang kasa*" *(Ch'ŏng Songgang kasa)* by Yi Annul (1571–1637) while "A Time to Drink" is followed by "On Passing Songgang's Tomb" *(Kwa Songgang myo)* by Kwŏn P'il.

There are two further manuscripts that contain some poems by Chŏng. The first, entitled *Sa miin kok ch'ŏp* (36.5 x 24.5 cm), consists of ten lines. Folds 1 through 5 contain Chinese translations of the two "Hymns"; folds 6 through 8 contain a postscript (1764) by Kim Sangsuk (1717–1792);and folds 9 and 10 contain the original texts of the two "Hymns." The second such edition, *Hyŏmnyul taesŏng,* consists of four chapters. The fourth chapter contains the text of "The Wanderings" with numerous variant readings.

The most complete collection of works by and on Chŏng Ch'ŏl is the *Songgang chŏnjip,* published by the Taedong Munhwa Yŏnguwŏn, Sŏnggyungwan University, in 1964. I have used the modern annotated edition of the *Pine River Anthology* by Kim Sayŏp, *Kyoju haeje Songgang kasa* (Seoul: Munhosa, 1955).

PAK ILLO

There are three editions of the *Collected Works of Pak Illo (Nogye chip).* The first was a woodblock printing in 1800; the second, again a woodblock edition, came out in 1904; the third, also in woodblock, was printed at an unknown date. The first chapter of the *Works* begins with the poet's family tree and diagrams on the *Doctrine of the Mean,* the *Great Learning,* and the *Elementary Learning.* The chapter also contains Chinese verse by Pak: rhymeprose; penta- and heptasyllabic quatrains; penta- and heptasyllabic *lü-shih;* old-style poetry. It also contains two prose works (1.16b–19b).

The second chapter, simply called an appendix, contains diverse examples of Chinese prose: memorials submitted by officials on Pak's behalf; a dirge; a biography; excerpts from the local gazetteer; epitaphs; invocations used for spring and autumn sacrifices; and others. The third chapter, the most important of the *Works,* contains sixty *sijo* and seven *kasa* poems in Korean. One curious feature about the second edition is that a *kasa* entitled "Tosan ka" appears at the very end of the *Works.* There are two reprints of the first edition, however, one of which has the text of "Tosan ka." The text used in this study lists "Tosan ka" in its table of contents (4b) though the poem does not appear in the body of the work. Poems 9–10 and 12–16 are in the manuscript copy, discovered in 1956, and poem 68 is in the *Taedong p'unga,* compiled and published in 1908 by Kim Kyohyŏn and added to Pak's canon in 1959. The photolithographic reprint of the *Works* was published by the Taedong Munhwa Yŏnguwŏn, Sŏnggyungwan University, in 1973. I have used the modern annotated edition, *Kaego Pak Nogye yŏngu,* by Yi Sangbo (Seoul: Ilchisa, 1962; expanded edition, Iu ch'ulp'ansa, 1980).

Yun Sŏndo

The *Collected Works of Yun Sŏndo (Kosan yugo)* comprises six chapters in woodblock and a chapter of chronological biography. King Chŏngjo ordered the governor of Chŏlla province to print the first six chapters. The first edition was printed in 1791 and the second in 1798. The chapter containing the chronology was reprinted in 1898.

Chapter 1 contains Yun's Chinese poetry—penta- and heptasyllabic *shih,* quatrains, and regulated verse. Chapter 2 contains sixteen memorials; chapter 3A, six additional memorials and essays on rites; chapters 3B, 4, and 5A, letters; chapter 5B, sacrificial speeches, offerings, village compact agreements, prefaces, records, discourses, epitaphs, opinions, and miscellany; and chapter 6A, more *shih* in Chinese, rhymeprose, treatises, examination questions, and memorials; and chapter 6B, poetry in Korean (1a–17b). The appendix contains an account of the posthumous epithet, a chronological biography, an inscription on the avenue to the grave, and postfaces to the *Works* by his descendants.

The *Works* in photolithographic reprint was issued by the Taedong Munhwa Yŏnguwŏn, Sŏnggyungwan University, in 1973. I have used the annotated editions by Yi Chaesu, *Yun Kosan yŏngu* (Seoul: Hagusa, 1955), and by Yun Sŏnggŭn, *Yun Sŏndo chakp'umjip* (Seoul: Hyŏngsŏl ch'ulp'ansa, 1982).

INDEX

ABOUT THE TRANSLATOR

Peter H. Lee is professor of Korean and comparative literature and chair of the Department of East Asian Languages and Cultures at the University of California, Los Angeles. His books include *Modern Korean Literature: An Anthology, A Korean Storyteller's Miscellany, Anthology of Korean Literature: From Early Times to the Nineteenth Century,* and other anthologies of classic and modern Korean poetry and prose in German and English.

STUDIES FROM THE
CENTER FOR KOREAN STUDIES

Studies on Korea: A Scholar's Guide, edited by Han-Kyo Kim. 1980.

Korean Communism, 1945–1980: A Reference Guide to the Political System, by Dae-Sook Suh. 1981

Korea and the United States: A Century of Cooperation, edited by Youngnok Koo and Dae-Sook Suh. 1984

The Reluctant Crusade: American Foreign Policy in Korea, 1941–1950, by James I. Matray. 1985

The Korean Frontier in America: Immigration to Hawaii, 1896–1910, by Wayne Patterson. 1988

Korean-American Relations: Documents Pertaining to the Far Eastern Diplomacy of the United States. Volume III. *The Period of Diminishing Influence, 1896–1905*, edited and with an introduction by Scott S. Burnett. 1989

Diplomacy of Asymmetry: Korean-American Relations to 1910, by Jongsuk Chay. 1990.

Pine River and Lone Peak: An Anthology of Three Chosŏn Dynasty Poets, translated, with an introduction, by Peter H. Lee. 1991.